Desperate to survive,
they were . . .

PLAYING FOR TIME

Arthur Miller's
Drama of the Holocaust

D1248851

Playing
for
Time

A Screenplay by
Arthur Miller

Based on the Book
by Fania Fénelon

BANTAM BOOKS
TORONTO · NEW YORK · LONDON

PLAYING FOR TIME
A Bantam Book / January 1981

ISBN 0-553-14547-9

Published simultaneously in the United States and Canada

*Bantam Books are published by Bantam Books, Inc. Its trade-
mark, consisting of the words "Bantam Books" and the por-
trayal of a bantam, is Registered in U.S. Patent and Trademark
Office and in other countries. Marca Registrada. Bantam
Books, Inc., 666 Fifth Avenue, New York, New York 10103.*

PRINTED IN THE UNITED STATES OF AMERICA

0 9 8 7 6 5 4 3 2 1

BOOK DESIGNED BY LURELLE CHEVERIE AND MIERRE

This screenplay is based on the facts in the book by the same title of Fania Fénelon, member of the Women's Orchestra in the Auschwitz-Birkenau Concentration Camp.

Playing
for
Time

Fade in on

Fania Fénelon singing. Her voice is unheard, we hear only the opening music.

Cut to

A sidewalk cafe in the afternoon. German soldiers relax, accompanied by French girls. We are in German Occupied Paris, 1942.

Cut to

The Nazi flag flying over Arc de Triomphe.

Cut to

In a cafe, Fania accompanies herself on the piano in a Parisian ballad warmed with longing and wartime sentiment. The audience, almost all German troops and French girlfriends, is well-behaved and enjoying her homey romanticism which salts their so-far epic conquests with pathos and a bit of self-pity.

Nothing in her manner betrays her hostility to Nazism and its destruction of France in the recent battles. She hopes they are enjoying their evening, promises to do what she can to help them forget their soldierly duties; but to the knowing eye there is perhaps a little extra irony in a look she casts, a smile she pours onto the upturned face of a nearby officer which suggests her inner turmoil at having to perform for the conqueror.

1

She is radiant here, an outgoing woman who is still young and with a certain heartiness and appetite for enjoyment.

She is roundly applauded now at the number's end, and she bows and backs into darkness.

Cut to

A train of freightcars, moving through open French farmland.

Cut to

The inside of one freightcar. It is packed with people, many of them well-dressed bourgeois, uncomfortably jammed in like this. The ordinariness of the types is emphasized, but above that their individuation. Moreover, while all are of course deeply uneasy and uncomfortable, there is no open alarm.

A husband is massaging his wife's cramped shoulders.

A mother is working to remove a speck from a teenage daughter's eye.

Worker types survey the mass with suspicions.

A *clochard*—a beggar woman off a Paris street wrapped in rags, and rather at home in this situation, surveys the company.

A 2nd mother pulls a young boy away from a neighbor's bag of food.

Chic people try to keep apart, soigné, even bored.

Students are trying to bury themselves in novels.

Two intellectuals are scrunched up on the floor, playing chess on a small board.

A boy scout of twelve who is doing his knots on a short rope.

An old asthmatic man in a fur collared coat is urged by his wife to take his pill. He holds it between his fingers, unhappily looking around for water.

Cut to

Fania, dressed in a beautiful fur coat and fur hat; her elegant valise is at her feet. She has a net with some fruit and a sausage, bread, and a bottle of water—and offers the old man a drink of it. He gratefully takes it, takes his pill, drinks a sip, and returns her the bottle.

Beside Fania on the straw-covered floor sits Marianne, a girl of twenty, quite well-dressed and overweight. Marianne has an unmarked, naive face. She is avidly glancing down at Fania's net.

FANIA

Have another piece of sausage, if you like.

MARIANNE

I'm so stupid—I never thought to take anything.

FANIA

(Kindly)

Well, I suppose your mother has always done that for you.

MARIANNE

Yes. Just a tiny piece . . .
(She breaks off more than a tiny piece.)

3

I still can't believe I'm sitting so close to you!
I have every one of your records, I think.
Really—all my friends love your style.

Marianne bites her sausage and chews sensually.

FANIA

Do you know why they arrested you?

MARIANNE
(Glances about nervously for an interloper)
I think it was because of my boyfriend—he's
in the Resistance.

FANIA

Oh! —Mine too.

MARIANNE
(Reaches under her coat)
I adore him! Maurice is his name.

She hands a snapshot to Fania who looks at it and
smiles admiringly. Then Fania opens her soft leather
purse and hands a snapshot to Marianne.

FANIA

He's Robert.

MARIANNE
(Looking at photo)
Oh, he's fantastic! —a blond! I love blonds.
(They return photos)
In the prison they keep beating me up....

FANIA

Me, too.

4

MARIANNE

... They kept asking where he is, but I don't even know! —They nearly broke this arm.
(Glancing around)
But somebody said it's really because we're Jewish that they picked us up. Are you?

FANIA

Half.

MARIANNE

I'm half too. Although it never meant anything to me.

FANIA

Nor me.

They silently stare at the others. Marianne glances down at Fania's food again.

FANIA

You really shouldn't eat so much.

MARIANNE

I can't help it; I never used to until the prison. It made me hungry all the time. I just hope my boyfriend never sees me like this—you wouldn't believe how slim I was only a few months ago. And now I'm bursting out of everything. But my legs are still good. Don't you think?
(She extends her leg rather childishly.)
I still can't believe I'm sitting next to you! I really have all your records.

Cut to

The boy scout who is now sitting with a compass on

5

his knee, studying the needle. Beside him, his mother is asleep.

FANIA

Can you tell our direction?

BOY SCOUT

South.

A nearby worker overhears.

WORKER

It's probably going to be Munich. They need labor on the farms around there.

2ND WORKER

I wouldn't mind. I love the outdoors.

A nearby woman adds her wisdom.

WOMAN

They have those tiny little thatched houses down there. I've seen photographs.

1ST CHESS PLAYER

In my opinion we'll be machine-gunned right where we sit—and I'm especially sorry for your sake, Madame Fenelon—your music is for me the sound of Paris.

FANIA

Thank you.

MARIANNE

(Quietly)
I'm not sure I could do farm work—could you?

6

FANIA

(Shrugs)
Have you ever worked?

MARIANNE

(A little laugh)
Oh no—I never even *met* a worker till the
prison. I was in school or at home all my life.
(The little laugh again.)
And now I don't even know where my parents
are. . . .
*(She verges on a shivering fear with star-
tling rapidity.)*
Would you mind if we sort of stuck together?

Fania puts an arm around her and Marianne nestles
gratefully into Fania's body. A moment passes; Fania
reaches into her net and gives Marianne a bonbon.
Marianne avidly eats it and Fania pats her hair as
though, in effect, forgiving her another dietary lapse.

Cut to

The boy scout, alert to some change in the compass,
takes it off his knee, shakes it, then sets it back on
his knee.

FANIA

Has it changed?

BOY SCOUT

We've turned to the east.

The 1st chess player turns to the scout, then leans
over to read compass himself. He then resumes his
position, a stare of heightened apprehension growing
on his face.

2ND CHESS PLAYER
(Reassuringly)
But a compass can't be right with so much
metal around it, can it?

Cut to

A sudden explosion of indignation from deep in the
crowd; people leaping up to escape something under
the hay on the floor; yells of disgust and anger. . . .
The mother and little boy emerge from within the
crowd, he buttoning his pants. . . .

MOTHER
Well what is he supposed to do!

1ST MAN
He can use the pail over there!

2ND MAN
That pail is full.

1ST MAN
*(He yells up to a grill high in a wall of the
car.)*
Hey! Let us empty the pail!

Only the sound of the clanking train returns. Defeated,
the deportees rearrange themselves to find dry places
on the floor. The train lurches.

Cut to

The slop pail, filled with the deportees' urine, over-
turning.

Cut to

People, with higher disgust, fleeing from the contents

8

and crowding each other even more, some even remaining on their feet.

Cut to

Marianne coming out of Fania's embrace, whispers in her ear, while placing a hand on her own stomach. Fania glances down at her with distress.

> FANIA
> Try to hold out—they'll *have* to open the doors soon.

> MARIANNE
> Could I have another sip of water?

> FANIA
> But only wet your mouth, not more. You've got to try to discipline yourself.

Marianne drinks from a mineral water bottle from Fania's net. Fania, as she is replacing the stopper, happens to catch the thirsty stare of the old asthmatic man. She hesitates, then holds out the bottle which is taken by the asthmatic's wife. The old man sips; he is weaker than earlier.

Cut to

The nearly full water bottle. Superimposed on it is the crowd in its present postures which are still rather normal for the circumstance—some are standing to avoid the floor, and the others are alert and have energy.

The water level lowers in the bottle as it is used; and the superimposed crowd is losing its energy, with people unconscious, one on top of the other, lips are parched, signs of real distress. ....

9

Cut to

Fania, asleep sitting up. Marianne awakens, lips parched, tries to get a drop out of the bottle but it is empty. She looks into Fania's net, but it too is empty. Only half alive, Marianne, expressionless, sees a fight starting near her as a man pushes a woman away—and the woman is lowering her dress. . . .

MAN

Do it over there! —this is *my* place!

The woman trips over someone, looks down. . . .

Cut to

The old asthmatic man. He's dead. His wife, spiritless and silent, holds his head in her lap.

Cut to

The faces of the deportees experiencing the presence of the dead man. Unable to bear it longer, Fania climbs up to the grill.

FANIA

HALLOO! Listen! We've got a dead man in here! HALLOO!

Surprisingly now, there is a squeal of brakes. People are thrown against each other, and the train stops.

Expectation, fear, hope . . .

Cut to

The freight car doors rolling open. A powerful searchlight bathes the crowd, blinding them. The people try to get to their feet and gather their belongings.

From outside, half a dozen kapos leap into the car—
these are prisoners working for the administration—
and, armed with truncheons, they pull people out of
the car onto the ground. ("Hurry up, everybody out,
get moving" . . . etc.) They are brutal, enjoying their
power.

Cut to

The debarkation area. Under the spectral arc lights
the cars are being emptied. Kapos are loading valises
onto trolleys, but with a certain care, like porters.

Cut to

The train platform. Late at night. Still wearing her fur
coat and hat, Fania half unwillingly gives up her valise
to a kapo. This kapo eyes Marianne's body and gives
her a toothless come-on smile.

Cut to

A sudden close up of Dr. Mengele. This monster, the
Angel of Death so-called, is a small, dapper man with
a not unattractive face. He is the physician in charge
of the Selections and in this shot is simply standing
at the edge of the milling crowd, observing the people.
Now he nods slightly, it is an order.

Cut to

SS guards pushing the people into a rough line, one
behind the other. A dozen or more guard dogs and
handlers keep the proceedings lively. Snarls electrify,
the air is filled with the whines of eager dogs. But the
violence is still controlled.

Dr. Mengele, facing the head of the line. With a gesture to right or left, with hardly a second's interval
between individuals, he motions people toward several

11

waiting trucks (which are marked with the Red Cross), or to an area where they stand and wait. The latter are generally stronger, male and younger.

And so the line moves rapidly toward Mengele's pointing fingers, and the crowd parts to the left and the right.

Cut to

Fania, right behind Marianne on line, speaks into her ear.

FANIA

> It's going to be all right—you see?—the Red Cross is here.

Cut to

People being loaded onto the open-backed trucks, which are marked with large Red Crosses. Babies are passed over the crowd to mothers, the aged are carried aboard with the stronger helping. The air still carries the whines and barks of the dogs, the sounds of hurried commands.

Once again, intermittent close shots individualize the crowd, the types, relationships. The crowd, in fact, is relieved to get aboard and moving to some destination.

Cut to

The trucks pulling away. Marianne and Fania, alone on the ground, look up at the packed truck which remains. Kapos raise its tailgate and fasten it.

FANIA

Wait—we're supposed to get on, aren't we?

KAPO

How old are you?

FANIA

I'm twenty-eight, she's twenty.

MARIANNE

I wouldn't mind a walk—may we?

KAPO
(The very faintest glimmer of humor—he too is exhausted, skinny. He gives his consent.)
You can walk.

The kapo hurries up ahead and boards the truck. The truck starts to pull away, leaving the two women behind.

Cut to

The people on the truck. The camera memorializes the faces we have come to know on the train—the boy scout, the chess players, boy scout's mother, etc. The truck moves off into darkness.

Cut to

Marianne and Fania as they look around at the darkness—shapes of dark buildings surround them. Down the track we hear the activity of the guards and those selected to live.

FANIA

I guess we follow the trucks.

The two move together into the darkness.

13

Cut to

A strange orange glow in the night sky. Is it a massive reflection of bright lights or is it flame? It comes from some half a mile off.

Cut to

Fania and Marianne walking, looking up at the glow.

FANIA
There must be some sort of factory.

Out of the darkness a kapo pops up and walks along with them. He is gaunt, puts an arm around Marianne.

KAPO
Listen . . . I'll give you coffee.

FANIA
(Pulling his arm away from Marianne)
This must be some high-class place—a cup of coffee for a woman?

KAPO
That's a lot.
(Points arrantly at Marianne)
See you later, Beauty.

Fania protectively grasps the frightened Marianne's hand and they move on into the dark toward the glow.

Cut to

The reception area. Fania and Marianne enter the dimly lit room, perhaps 20 × 40. They enter in uncertainly, unsure if they're supposed to be here. Five Polish women prisoners, employed here, are lounging around a table. One cleans her nails, another reads a

14

scrap of newspaper, another is combing her companion's long hair. They are hefty, coarse, peasant types.

FANIA

> (After a moment)
> Is this where we get our things back?

She asks this question because—as we see now—along one wall of this room and extending out into a corridor which leads deeper into the building are, in neat piles, hundreds and hundreds of valises, stacks of clothes, piles of shoes, bins full of spectacles, false teeth, underwear, sweaters, gloves, galoshes, and every other imaginable article of clothing.

The Polish women turn to Fania and Marianne. One of them beckons silently, and the two approach her.

From the corridor enter two SS women in uniform. One of them is Frau Schmidt, the brutal, stupid German supervisor of the operation. They halt and expressionlessly observe.

The first Polish woman stands from the table, and simply takes Fania's handbag out of her hand. The second Polish woman grabs hold of Fania's fur coat collar and pulls it off her. Bag and coat go into the hands of the SS women who admiringly examine them.

FIRST POLISH WOMAN

> Your shoes.

Fania and Marianne, both in fear now, remove their shoes, which are carried to Frau Schmidt by the Poles. Frau Schmidt examines the expensive shoes appreciatively.

15

Undress.

Cut to

Fania and Marianne sinking into a stunned astonishment. And now hands working scissors enter the shot. Their hair—Fania has braids which are hard to cut—is totally removed, leaving tufts.

Cut to

A long number 346991 being tattooed on an arm. Backing, we see it is Marianne's arm: she is now in ludicrously outsized dress and shoes far too large. The same for Fania who is staring down at her own tattoo. The tattooer is a male kapo, who works with his tongue sticking out the corner of his mouth.

Cut to

A hundred or so women being handed dresses, worn out and sometimes mere shreds. Others are having their hair shorn as they wait to be tattooed. SS women move about, in charge.

Cut to

Frau Schmidt, who is handed the little chess set from the train; she admires it as well as the boy scout's compass. She sets them on the counter. They are then placed by a Polish woman in a receptacle already loaded with toys, stuffed animals, soccer balls, sports things.

Cut to

Fania, nearby, as she recognizes these relics; her eyes flare with terror. She turns toward a nearby window.

16

Cut to

The window. We see the eerie glow in the sky.

Cut to

One of the Polish women, all but finished pinning Fania's plaits on her own hair, imitating Fania's sophisticated walk as her sister workers laugh.

Fania, humiliated and angered, touches her bare scalp. She looks out the window.

Cut to

The workgang, from Fania's point of view. An exhausted woman collapses at the feet of Lagerfuhrerin Maria Mandel, who gestures toward a wheelbarrow. As kapos carry the woman, one of her arms brushes Mandel's coat. Mandel viciously hits the arm away, brushing off her coat sleeve as the woman is dumped into the wheelbarrow.

Inside the reception area.

> POLISH WOMAN
> How do I look, Jew-Crap?

> FANIA
> I'm not Jew-Crap, I'm French!

An uproar of laughter, and out of nowhere a smashing slap knocks Fania reeling to the floor. Over her stands SS Frau Schmidt, a powerhouse, looking down with menace.

Dissolve to dark

Cut to

The quarantine block—this is the barracks; dimly lit by a hanging bulb or two; a corridor between shelves, in effect, where women lie with barely room between each shelf to turn over; the shelves go to the ceiling.

Fania and Marianne enter the corridor, left there by a Polish woman, the Blockawa or Block Warden. She gestures for them to take bunks above and starts to turn to leave.

The women in the bunks are cadaverous, barely able to summon interest in these new arrivals.

> FANIA
>
> Where are the people we came with?—they went off on the trucks. . . ?

The Blockawa grips her arm and leads her to a window and points out.

Cut to

The orange sky-glow. But from this closer distance smoke can be seen rising from a tall stack.

Cut to

Fania, Marianne and the Blockawa. The Blockawa points upward through the window.

> BLOCKAWA
>
> Your friends. You see? —cooking. You too, pretty soon.

The Blockawa cutely blinks both eyes, grins reassuringly, and walks away.

Cut to

Marianne, quietly sobbing as she lies beside Fania on their bunk.

FANIA

Marianne? Listen to me. Come, girl, stop that.

MARIANNE

Why are they doing this? What do they get from it?

Fania glances to her other side where, asleep on the shelf beside her, lies a famished looking woman who might well be dead.

FANIA
(Turning back to Marianne)
I've always had to have an aim in life—something I wanted to do next. That's what we need now if we're ever to get out of here alive.

MARIANNE

What sort of an aim?

Fania looks down into the corridor below at the Blockawa, on patrol with a truncheon in her fist.

FANIA

If I ever get out of here alive, I'm going to kill a Polish woman.

Fania lies back, shuts her eyes, hating herself a little.

MARIANNE

I'm so hungry Fania. Hold me.

Fania embraces Marianne; then she turns the other way to look at the woman on her other side; she is skeletal, absolutely still. Cautiously Fania touches her skin and draws her hand away at the cold touch. Then she gives her a little shake. The woman has died.

Now she leans over the edge of the bunk and calls to the Blockawa.

FANIA

There's a dead woman up here.

The Blockawa, club in hand, allows a moment to pass; she slowly looks up at Fania with the interest of a seal, then strolls away.

Cut to

A close shot of Fania and Marianne in their bunk. Marianne stares in fright at the corpse, then hides her face in Fania's side.

FANIA

We must have an aim. And I think the aim is to try to remember everything. I'll tell you a story—once upon a time there was a prince named Jean and he was terribly handsome. And he married a princess named Jeannette and she was terribly beautiful.

Marianne comes out of hiding under Fania's arm—she is childishly interested. . . .

MARIANNE

And?

FANIA

And one day the prince said, "My dear, we must have an aim in life, we must make children," and so they. . . .

20

As Fania talks, slowly fade to a double exposure of Fania and Marianne. Snow falls over the image of the two women in their bunk: a forest; now spring comes; flowers appear and green grass; brook ice melts— always over the image of Fania and Marianne dragging stones, carrying wood, digging drainage ditches. . . . And finally, once again, in their bunk—now without the dead woman, and they are both asleep, side by side. And both are haggard now, with the half-starved look of the other prisoners.

A voice blares out: "ATTENTION!"

Cut to

The barracks. Women start to come obediently out of their bunks into the corridor. The Blockawa yells.

> BLOCKAWA
> Remain in place! Does anybody know how to sing *Madame Butterfly!*

Astonished silence. The Blockawa infuriates herself.

> BLOCKAWA
> Does anyone know how to sing *Madame Butterfly!*

Cut to

Fania, unsure whether to volunteer; glances at Marianne who urges her silently to do so. Below in the corridor the Blockawa starts to leave. Fania suddenly lunges and, half hanging out the bunk, waves to the monster woman. . . .

> FANIA
> I can!

Cut to

Fania entering from exterior darkness into a lighted room. She halts, looking around in total astonishment.

Cut to

The musicians' barrack dayroom. Fania, as in a wild dream, sees some 25 women, most seated behind music stands, badly but cleanly dressed; some with shaved heads (Jewesses), others still with their hair. Unlike her former barracks with faint and few light bulbs, there is brightness here, although it is actually quite bare of furniture.

In center stands a Beckstein grand, shiny, beautiful. At sight of the piano, Fania's mouth falls open.

Compared to these women Fania is indeed woebegone—dirty, in ludicrously enormous shoes, torn and ill-fitting dress.

Elzvieta, an older Pole with a full head of hair, approaches Fania, and with a wet cloth wipes her face. Fania regards this kindness incredulously. Now Elzvieta runs her pitying fingers down Fania's cheek.

Etalina, petite, Roumanian, 18, brings a lump of bread and puts it in Fania's hand.

> ETALINA
> I'm Etalina. I saw you in Paris once, at the "Melody."
> *(Fania bites into the bread.)*
> My parents took me there last year for my birthday—I was seventeen.

Michou enters the group; a tiny determined girl of 20, a militant communist, terribly pale, with a soft poetic

22

voice. Etalina indicates her—(not without a slight air of joking superciliousness toward this wraith).

ETALINA

But she's the one who recognized you. This is Michou.

MICHOU

I saw you yesterday coming out of your barracks and I ran and told our kapo—she promised to audition you—

FANIA

What audition?

ETALINA

For the orchestra—us.
(With some awe)
Our conductor is Alma Rosé.
(Calls offscreen)
Laure, come and meet Fania Fénelon!
(To Fania)
She's one of our best players, but she's shy as a deer. She can do Bach solos....

LAURE

(Enters shot. Almost a whisper as she curtsies)
I'm honored to meet you.

FANIA

How do you do, Laure.
(To Etalina)
Rosé? —there was a string quartet by that name....

MICHOU

Alma is the first violinist's daughter.

FANIA

Then her uncle must be Gustav Mahler . . .
the composer. . . .

ELZVIETA

Yes; she has a fantastic talent. . . .

ETALINA

But not a warm heart, be careful. . . .

Michou touches Etalina to shush her, looking offscreen.

Cut to

Alma Rosé, as she makes her entrance—there is instant silence and respect. Now three Blockawas—
Polish prisoners acting as police in effect, and all
weighty types—appear and look on with belligerent
curiosity. (They don't approve this coddling of Jews,
in fact.)

Alma comes to the group, addressing Fania: She is
thin, extremely Germanic, scrubbed clean, her shabby
clothes brushed. Her face shows her determination,
even fanatical perfectionism, her only defense here.

ALMA

You are Mademoiselle Fenelon?

FANIA

Yes, Madame.

ALMA

You play the piano?

FANIA

Oh yes, Madame!

24

The fervor of her voice causes an excited giggle among some of the onlookers.

ALMA
Let me hear something from *Madame Butter-fly*.

Alma goes to a chair, sits; others arrange themselves.

Fania approaches the fabulous piano; it is all like a dream—she is sloughing along in these immense mens' shoes, a fuzz of hair on her bald head, her face gaunt from near starvation diet—and she sits before the keys and can't help bending over and kissing them. She starts to play *Un bel di* . . .

Cut to

Fania's hands. They are crusted with filth, nails broken. She is stiff and strikes a double note.

Cut to

Fania, at the piano. She stops, blows on her fingers. Now she plays and sings. After two bars . . .

Cut to

The group. All are glancing at Alma's reaction—she is quickened, eager to claim Fania for her orchestra.

Cut to

Fania. In her face and voice, confident now and warm, are the ironic longings for the music's life-giving love-liness. The mood is shattered by the sounds of the scraping of chairs and people suddenly standing. Fania turns, stops playing.

Cut to

Lagerführerin Mandel entering the dayroom; she is
Chief of the Women's Section of the entire camp.
About 28, tall, blonde, shining with health, beautiful
in her black uniform. Musicians, Blockawas, all are
standing at rigid attention before her. Fania sees this,
and attempts to do likewise—although only half suc-
cessfully in her state of semi-shock.

MANDEL

At ease.

She comes and examines Fania, head to foot. And to
Alma...

MANDEL

You will take her.

ALMA

Yes, Frau Lagerführerin, certainly—she is
very good.

MANDEL
(Facing Fania)
She is wonderful.

There is something competitive in Alma's face.

MANDEL

Do you know any German music?

FANIA
(Hesitates, her eyes lowered in trepidation.)
Yes...

MANDEL

... I am Lagerführerin Maria Mandel, in command of all women in this camp.

(*Nods in deference*)

I . . . had forgotten to tell Madame Rosé . . . that I really can't join the orchestra . . . unless my friend #346991 is admitted also—she has a beautiful voice.

(*Now she meets Mandel's surprised look.*)
She is in Barracks B.

(*Mandel is silent; surprised actually.*)
Without her, I . . . must refuse . . . I'm sorry.

Absolute astonishment strikes the expressions of the other musicians.

Cut to

Mandel, who holds on Fania for an additional moment, her mind unreadable.

Cut to

The kapos, furious, but more incredulous than anything else.

Cut to

Fania and Tchaikowska, a kapo, hurrying down a camp "street"—(a corridor between barracks buildings). Fania is urging Tchaikowska to go faster . . . they turn the corner of a building and come upon about twenty women who are being driven by club-wielding Blockawas. Many of these women are near death, falling down, crawling.

In complete contrast, in the background, Mala comes to a halt; with her an SS officer. She is a tall, striking Jewess, wears the Star. But—oddly enough—there is no subservience in her manner but rather a seriousness and confidence. She carries a thick notebook.

Marianne is being pulled and struck by a Blockawa whose pressure she is resisting, as she tries to get back into the barracks building.

FANIA
(To Tchaikowska, pointing)
That's her! Quick! Marianne. . . !

Fania drops behind the kapo Tchaikowska—who has the authority here and who walks up to the Blockawa.

TCHAIKOWSKA
Frau Lagerführerin wants this one.

Marianne nearly faints into Fania's arms as they start to move away from the surprised Blockawa and the deadened, staggering group of women.

Cut to

Marianne, her face still smudged with dirt, deep scratches on her neck. Incredibly enough she is still singing to Fania's piano accompaniment in the musicians' barracks.

Cut to

Mandel, legs sheathed in silk, her cap off, letting her blonde hair fall to her shoulders. She listens. Alma stands a deferential few paces behind her. And in the background, the musicians, all listening.

Fania is playing encouragingly, glancing from time to time up at Marianne to urge her on. Marianne has a fevered look in her eyes, she is singing for her life. The song ends. Silence.

MANDEL
(To Alma)
Get them dressed.

Cut to

Marianne who starts to sway but is held up by Fania.

Cut to

A counter; behind it from floor to ceiling the clothing of the dead.

Blockawas, and the Chief here—Frau Schmidt—stand rigidly at attention. Mandel is holding up a brassiere which she places over Marianne's large breasts. Then gives it to Marianne. Now she takes a pair of fine silk panties, holds them up for Fania, who accepts them.

> MANDEL
> *(To Frau Schmidt)*
> Find shoes that fit her.

> FRAU SCHMIDT
> Of course.
> *(To Fania)*
> They look very small, what size are they?

> FANIA
> Four.

> FRAU SCHMIDT
> *(To Mandel)*
> I doubt very much that we have ...

> MANDEL
> Feet must be warm and comfortable or the voice is affected. Find them for my little singer.

Frau Schmidt is irritated but obedient.

Fania and Marianne are thankful to Mandel, but what is the meaning of this incredible insistence?

Mandel exits, leaving Frau Schmidt rummaging in the bin full of womens' shoes.

A Blockawa sweeps a woolen coat off the counter and furiously throws it at Fania who blocks it with her arm.

While Frau Schmidt continues to search, Fania's eye transforms the pile of shoes.

Dissolve to

Women's legs walking on a railroad station platform. In effect, the shoes come alive on the wearers' feet and move about on a sidewalk.

Cut to

Alma, tapping on her podium with her baton, raising her arms to begin a number; the orchestra is ready. Suddenly eyes catch something off camera and everyone springs to their feet and at attention.

Mandel enters, followed by her orderly. Mandel is carrying a box full of shoes, four or five pair.

Cut to

Mandel. Her eyes are happy, somehow softened.

MANDEL
Sit down here, Fania.

Fania comes to her from the piano bench, sits before her at her gestured command. Mandel sets the box of shoes down, takes out a pair of fur-lined boots—and kneels before Fania!

Fania is now torn; she dares not turn back these incredible attentions, at the same time she fears what

30

accepting them may imply for her future. She looks down at the fur boot in Mandel's hand. . . .

Cut to

A close shot of the boot. The camera either vivifies this boot, gives it the life of its deceased owner—or actually fills it with a leg, and we see the pair of boots on living legs . . . perhaps walking on a city street.

Cut to

Mandel, rising to her feet as Fania stands in the fur boots. She looks up from them to Mandel's pleased face and can't help resolving her conflict by saying. . . .

FANIA
Dankeschön Frau Lagerführerin.

Cut to

Mandel. Her pleasure flows onto her face; there is an element of masterly dominance in her expression, and some sort of affection, in fact.

Cut to

The entire orchestra, rehearsing. Fania has hands poised over the keyboard; Alma, baton raised, starts the piece—an orchestral number of von Suppé. The sound is not quite horrible, but very nearly. The forty-odd players, apart from some of them being totally inadequate, are distressed by hunger and fear and never quite keep the number from collapsing.

Cut to

The orchestra. The camera introduces us to the main supporting characters:

31

Elzvieta, a very good violinist, a rather aristocratic Pole who, as a non-Jew, still has her hair.

Paulette, a woman in her twenties, German-Jewish, an excellent cellist, who is presently pained by the bad playing of her compatriot beside her, who is . . .

Liesle, a bony, timid, near-hysterically frightened mandolin player, trying desperately to keep up with the beat. Belgian.

Laure, violinist, fine player, slim and noble-looking, Belgian, extremely intelligent, poetic face.

Etalina, a wisecracker, small, Roumanian, violinist, a tomboy.

Michou, French, plays the flute.

Further in the background of the story are . . .

Giselle, a freckled, very young French girl who can barely play the concertina at all, but is too young to despair, and thus squeezes as loudly as possible.

Berta, a teacher.

Varya, cymbals. A Pole who has her hair.

Katrina, Polish, a very bad guitarist, stubborn, unteachable; has her hair.

Olga, Ukrainian accordionist, a dumbbell who will later take over the orchestra.

Greta, Dutch accordionist, country girl, naive and scared at all times; very poor player.

Esther, a taut, militant Zionist who bears in her intense eyes the vision of Palestine; drummer.

Tchaikowska, leading kapo.

From time to time, one or more of the secondary characters will emerge on the foreground of this story in order to keep alive and vivid the sense that the "background group" is made of individuals. If this film is to approach even an indication of the vastness of the human disaster involved, the minor characters will have to be kept dramatically alive even in shots where they are only seen and don't have lines.

Cut to

Alma, tapping angrily on the podium ... the orchestra breaks off.

> **ALMA**
> Why is it so loud? This is not band music, we are not playing against the wind—why can you not obey my instructions!
> *(A note of futile and somehow dangerous anxiety on the verge of real anger.)*
> Music is the holiest activity of mankind, you must apply yourselves day and night, you must listen to yourselves, you must aspire to some improvement. . . . ! You cannot simply repeat the same mistakes. . . .

She can't go on, and simply walks hurriedly out of the room to recover herself. For a moment, the women keep an abashed silence.

> **ETALINA**
> At ease, Philharmonic.

The women set down their instruments and stand and stretch. . . . Etalina comes to Fania at the piano.

I think you've upset her—your being so good;
she suddenly heard what we really sound like.

Paulette enters the shot and Liesle. Then Giselle.

FANIA

Well it *was* a bit loud. . . .

PAULETTE

(Of Liesle)
She can't learn that number—we've got to
go loud or she's had it.

LIESLE

(Defensively, a whine)
I only studied less than six months in my
whole life.

ETALINA

And that's the smartest six months *you* ever
spent.
(To Fania)
It's not her altogether—it's the Maestro herself who's brought on this trouble.

FANIA

Why?

ETALINA

We were simply a marching band when we
started—we'd play the prisoners out to their
work assignments. But Alma got ambitious
and the first thing you know we're doing these
orchestral numbers, giving concerts for the
high brass . . . playing Beethoven, for God's
sake. She's a victim of her own pride and
we're in trouble now.

MARIANNE
(Entering the shot)
Do we ever get dinner?

LIESLE
(Laughs)
Listen to her. . . !

ETALINA
The slops'll be here any time now, dear.

FANIA
Why, trouble, Etalina?

ETALINA
Because once the big shots started coming to hear us they began getting bored hearing the same three numbers.

PAULETTE
We have no other orchestrations. . . .

ETALINA
And no composer ever wrote for this idiotic kind of instrumentation. I mean, piccolos, guitars, flutes, violins, no bass, no horns, no . . .

MICHOU
(To Fania)
You don't orchestrate, do you?

Obviously Fania doesn't, but her mouth opens and her eyes are inventing. . . .

PAULETTE
I'm really getting worried—we've done practically the same concert at least a dozen times.

The Commandant sometimes doesn't even stay to the end.

MARIANNE
(Her frightened eyes turn to Fania.)
But you do know how to orchestrate, Fania!
(Fania looks into her scared face.)
And then they could play all sorts of things!

FANIA
...Actually...
(To the women)
I can.

ETALINA and PAULETTE
Orchestrate???

FANIA
Well yes ... not professionally, but I ...

MICHOU
I knew it!

Paulette swerves about and yells to the women.

PAULETTE
She can orchestrate!

Etalina and Paulette instantly take off down the length of the room flanked by a dozen women all cheering and talking ... and come to Alma's door where Etalina knocks.

Cut to

Alma's room. Alma is sitting by a window, baton still in her grip. Etalina and Paulette step into the room.

We thought you'd want to know, Madame—
Fania Fenelon knows how to orchestrate.

The importance of this news is evident in Alma's expression. She stands. Fania is brought forward and into the room.

ALMA

(To the others)
Leave us. Leave us, please.

She shuts the door on the women. The last face we see is Marianne's, imploring Fania to press on. Alma gestures to the bed where Fania sits as Alma sits on the chair facing her. Fania looks around at the clean bare room.

ALMA

Tell me the truth, Fania.

FANIA

Yes, I can— I don't see why not.

ALMA

And I suppose you . . . actually studied?

FANIA

(Plunging on)
At the Paris Conservatory.

ALMA

Oh, Fania—what luck! What luck to have you!
There's been a terrible pressure on me for
some weeks now . . . for something new. . . .

FANIA

So they tell me. . . .

37

ALMA

I'm so exhausted and rushed that I've simply
been unable to, myself. Could you start
with. . . ?
    (She picks up piano music from a table.)
I have a piano score for *Carmen.* . . .

FANIA

Well, I suppose yes, I could do *Carmen.* . . .

ALMA

Or something German . . . here's another von
Suppé. . . .

FANIA

I can't bear von Suppé. . . .

ALMA

I know, but they adore anything by von Suppé
and we must try to please them, Fania.
    (Their eyes meet. Alma is a mite defensive,
    but it comes out with strength.)
. . . Well that is elementary, it seems to me.

FANIA

I suppose. But I prefer to think that I am
saving my life rather than trying to please
the SS.

ALMA

And you think you can do one without the
other?

Fania shuts up; clearly it is a dilemma; but she is also
not trusting Alma. Now Alma relents.

ALMA

You'll begin immediately.

FANIA

I'll need people to copy the parts . . . and
music paper.

ALMA

We can't possibly get music paper. . . .

FANIA

Couldn't you request some?

ALMA

There is a war on, my dear!

Suddenly, in this exclamation is Alma's *own* German
indignation.

ALMA

Come—I'll find paper, and you and the girls
can draw the lines yourself.
   (*Fania rises, goes past her to the door.*)
Fania?
   (*Fania turns to her, a slight smile.*)
I can't help striving for perfection; I was
trained that way, I can't change now.

FANIA

Madame, I'm hardly in a position to criticize
you when I am also trying to please.

ALMA

Exactly—but we are artists, we can't help
that; you have nothing to be ashamed of.
   (*Alma now comes to Fania—and in a more
   confessing, intimate tone . . .*)
Please try to hurry the work—they're so very
changeable toward us, you see? Something
new and surprising would be . . .
   (*Her fear is outright, open.*)

39

. . . a tremendous help. So you'll be quick, Fania?

Cut to

Fania. Her eyes are filling with terror and determination. . . .

Cut to

The dayroom, that evening. A concert is in full swing for the Commandant Kramer and Dr. Mengele, primarily—but other officers are here too, including Frau Schmidt and Lagerführerin Mandel, forming an audience of perhaps twenty.

Madame Alma Rosé, face aglow, is apprehensively conducting, pushing the stone uphill.

The camera detects the players' abilities—the few good ones trying to overflow onto the sounds of the shaky ones.

Kramer, Dr. Mengele and Mandel are naturally seated in the front "row." Mandel is interested, Dr. Mengele, who knows music, is very attentive, also amused; Kramer, a bull-necked killer, is struggling to keep his eyes open.

The number is ending with a flashy run on the piano by Fania.

Alma turns and bows as though before a gigantic audience.

ALMA

And now, with your permission, *Meine Damen und Herrn*—a bit of popular music by our new member, Fania Fenelon.

Fania accompanies herself, singing a smoky, very Parisian ballad. And as she sings . . .

Dissolve to

Dr. Mengele, his face superimposed on Fania. Then we see him with finger raised, directing deportees emerging from a freight car to right and left, death or life. *Flames reflect orange light on his face.*

This gives way to . . .

A close up of Mengele. He seems actually attracted to Fania's voice and music.

Cut to

Fania, finishing her number—her face is tortured, but she is singing, fully, beautifully, to the finish.

Cut to

The audience. Fania takes bows, her eyes trying to evade the monsters' appreciation of her.

Cut to

Fania, dowsing her face with water as though trying to wash herself clean.

Cut to

The dormitory. Marianne is drawing out a box from under her bed—she opens it, takes out a package of margarine, starts to dig some out with a finger—and looks up guiltily, her finger nearly in her mouth.

Fania is standing nearby, having discovered her. Fania is still drying herself.

41

FANIA

Why do you steal when you know I can't stand margarine?

Marianne starts to put the margarine back in the box. Fania comes and forces it back into her hand. Fania's voice is losing its control.

Other women look up from their beds, still others are entering the dormitory—and gradually all are drawn to this.

FANIA

Anything you want of mine I wish you would simply take, Marianne!
(Turning to the other women)
And that goes for everyone—I don't want to keep anything from anyone who wants it. . . . And I hope you'll do the same for me if I'm desperate.

ETALINA

But Fania, we can't very well share everything.

FANIA

I refuse to turn into an animal for a gram of margarine or a potato peel!

PAULETTE

You don't mean share with the Poles too, though.

Fania hesitates . . . glances down the dormitory where half a dozen Polish women stand about—heavy, tough, their contempt evident despite their curiosity of the moment. (Katrina: Beefy, appalling guitarist. Varya: Athlete, shrewd, cymbals.)

42

ETALINA

Count me out, dear—those are monsters; even here in the same hell as we are, they're just praying every one of us goes to the gas. You share with those bitches, not me.

ELZVIETA
(A delicate, gentle Pole, beautiful head of hair.)
We're not all like that.

Slight pause.

PAULETTE

You just have a pet Jew—you like Fania, but you're an anti-Semite, Elzvieta.

ELZVIETA
(Timidly)
But I really am not. My father was an actor; we had a lot of Jewish friends in the theater. —I'm really not, Fania.
(Glancing at the satiric Etalina)
In my opinion, Etalina—
(With a glance toward the Poles)
they think that you people are probably going to be ... you know ...

ETALINA

Gassed. —You can say it, dear.

ELZVIETA

Well the point is that they want to feel superior because they'll probably live to go home, when the war ends ... being Gentiles.
(To Fania)
They're more stupid than evil.

FANIA

Then we should try to teach them.

After the first shock, Etalina laughs. Then another and
another until, with glances toward the stolid, suspi-
cious and bovine Poles, the whole gang are laughing
their heads off; and finally the Poles too join in.

GISELLE
*(A freckled-faced, red-haired Parisian tom-
boy)*
To hell with this—tell us about Paris—when
were you there last? What are they wearing?

Women gather around.

PAULETTE
Where are the skirts now?

FANIA
(Indicating. . . .)
Oh, to here,
(The knee)
but very full—the girls look like flowers.

MARIANNE
The heels are very high—the legs look terrific.
You can't buy stockings so they paint their
legs. My mother wouldn't let me, though.

PAULETTE
And the hair? —there were some women in a
convoy the other day—I think from Holland—
curls on top of their heads. . . .

FANIA
In Paris too—piled up top-curls. —Where
are those women?

44

ETALINA

They're burned up by now, I guess. What about songs? —you know any new ones?

FANIA

(To Etalina)
The way you say that, Etalina ...

ETALINA

Why not say it? We'll be better prepared for it when our time comes.

GISELLE

(Insistently)
Talk about Paris, Fania ...

LIESLE

Are they still playing swing?

FANIA

Are you Parisian?

LIESLE

No. But we went there for a vacation just before the war—play us some of the new songs, will you?

OTHERS

That's a great idea. . . . Come on, Fania. . . . Do you know "Stormy Weather?" . . . What was the name of your nightclub? . . . Did you make many records? . . . She's really famous, you know. . . .

The group moves out into the dayroom.

MICHOU

Can you play by ear? . . . come, sit down . . .

Fania sits at the piano, Marianne beside her . . .
when . . .

Cut to

Shmuel, in prisoner's stripes. He is an electrician, now
taping a wire along a wall of the dayroom. He is 45,
perhaps deranged, perhaps extraordinarily wise, it's
hard to say. He's like a little toy animal, large eyes,
curly hair, desperately shy. He makes little peeking
glances at the assembling women, but there's some air
of persistence about him, too.

Cut to

Fania, who senses some indecipherable communica-
tion from him and lets her gaze linger on him for an
instant. Then she breaks away and begins to play the
intro for "Stormy Weather."

After the first couple of lines, Marianne interrupts,
unable to restrain herself even though she is breaking
up Fania's number.

MARIANNE
Could I, Fania? Please?

Fania is quite astonished, looks at her with an embarrassed smile to cover her own resentment.

MARIANNE
I just have such a yen for it suddenly! Do you
mind?

Fania, embarrassed, shrugs and obliges, accompanying
Marianne, who sings the number—but "appealingly,"
sentimentally, where Fania sang intelligently, suavely.

46

Cut to

The Polish women. They are identifiable, in part, by the fact that they all have hair. They have come out of the dormitory and gather a little apart, and are pleasurably listening.

And before the music has a chance to die on Marianne's number, Fania picks up another, singing herself.

Camera pans the women's faces . . . maybe two dozen clustered around the piano . . . shorn, gaunt captives, yet this music brings up their lust to live and a certain joy. . . .

A chorus of players picks up a lyric and joins Fania, singing all together.

Cut to

Alma Rosé. Her door opens onto the dayroom, and she is about to protest the noise . . . but her gesture aborts and she stiffly concedes the moment, turns and goes back into her room, shutting the door.

Cut to

The next morning, outside in the camp "street." About 20 players form up outside the musicians' barracks. Each wears a bandanna, a uniform-like element, and of course the Jewesses have the yellow Star of David on their clothing. The Gentiles are indiscriminately mixed, perhaps four or five of them, identifiable mainly by their hair.

It is gray, just before dawn, very cold. Fania is in place at one corner of the formation; Alma Rosé appears from the barracks, sees her and halts.

ALMA

You don't have to do this, you're not in the band.

FANIA

I would like to see it . . . if it's not forbidden.

Alma is surprised, then shrugs, goes around to the head of the formation, raises her baton; and this crazy band, with no horns but with fiddles, flutes, accordian, guitars and cymbals, goes marching off behind Alma, who marches like a Prussian.

Cut to

The camp "square." The band is playing "stirring" march music on a low bandstand. Before them in blocks of five square stand the women prisoners about to go off to work.

Some of them are ill, supported by a neighbor's hand; some are fiercely erect, some old, some teenagers— their shoes don't match, some feet are wrapped in rags, and their clothes are ripped rags.

Cut to

A close shot of Fania. Her gaze has moved to a point . . . which is . . .

An angry prisoner.

This woman has caught Fania's eye and mimes spitting at her in contempt.

Cut to

Fania, quickly lowering her eyes.

48

Cut to

SS men, some handling attack dogs, ordering the prisoners to march. The whole mass moves across the mud.

SS OFFICER
(A whip against his boot beating time.)
Ein, zwei, drei . . . hup, hup, hup. . . !

Cut to

Fania lifting her eyes, forcing herself to watch. Suddenly up to her ear comes Shmuel. Frightened, surprised, she turns to him swiftly.

SHMUEL

   (Wild-eyed)
   Live!

He quickly limps away, his tool box on his shoulder.

Cut to

The dayroom. Women, lining paper with pencils and straightedges, are spread out around Fania near a window. Outside the gray light of winter afternoon.

Laure, a good violinist, is practicing some distance away—a Bach chaconne.

Marianne is staring out a window nearby, thinking of food.

Fania is seated, studying a piano score, pencil poised over a lined sheet on which a few notes have been set down. She is intense—worried?

Liesle is repeating the same three bars on her mandolin, with the same mistakes.

GISELLE

(Musing to no one in particular)
Imagine! —Painting their legs! I'd love
THAT....

Etalina passes behind Fania and, glancing down at
the few notes she has written, halts, surprised.

ETALINA

Is that all you've done?
(Fania glances up defensively)
Christ, at this rate we'll need another Hun-
dred Years War to get a score out of you.

Laure enters the shot, carrying her violin.

LAURE

Will you stop bothering her? Orchestrating
is tough work even for experts.

Alma comes out of her room, comes over to Fania
and looks down at the sheet. Then she looks at Fania
with real surprise.

ALMA

I have to speak to you.

Alma goes out into her room. Fania stands, as she
follows her out sees ...

The Polish women, triumphantly laughing—(softly,
though)—and pointing at her and miming her de-
capitation.

Cut to

Alma's room.

ALMA

Then you lied? —you can't orchestrate at all, can you.

FANIA

I'm quite able to do it; I'm sure I can.

ALMA

—What is it, then?

FANIA

One of the women this morning—spat at me.

ALMA

(Not understanding)
Yes?

FANIA

... I hadn't realized ... how they must hate us.

ALMA

Oh. Yes, of course; what did you expect?

FANIA

Well I ... I just hadn't thought about it.

ALMA

(Now sensing some remote criticism of her own character, she angers.)
Perhaps you are too conscientious a person for the orchestra ...

FANIA

No-no, I didn't mean ...

ALMA

If you'd be happier back in "B" Barracks ...

51

Madame, please—I wasn't criticizing you;
(*Unstrung*)
I'm just not used to being hated like that.

ALMA
(*Decisively*)
Fania—there is life or death in this place,
there is no room for anything else whatever.
—I intend to rehearse that piece tomorrow; I
want the parts by morning. If you are able,
that is. Are you?

FANIA
(*Defeated; yet, determined.*)
Yes, Madame.

She walks angrily past Alma out the door.

Cut to

The dayroom. Through the window nearby we see
darkness of night. Reflection of a big searchlight which
revolves somewhere beyond our line of sight, a rhythm
of this flashing light.

Fania at the piano is alone, working out the orchestration. She tries a chord. There is the jarring sound of
three rifle shots. She looks up, waits; then silence.
Someone probably got killed. She plays the chord
again; writes notes.

From outside we hear the hair-raising screeching of
someone being destroyed—and the shouts of men
killing. Then silence. Fania is in sharp conflict with
herself; she knows she is walling herself up against
all this. Steels herself again. Plays the chord. Can't
continue. Gets up, walks past dormitory doorway. She
looks in.

Cut to

The dormitory, at night. The whole orchestra, some forty, asleep in beds.

Cut to

Fania, in the dayroom, passing the dormitory door, goes into a dark narrow corridor at the end of which is a door. She opens this door. . . .

Cut to

The toilet. On the toilet bowl Marianne is straddling a man, a kapo still wearing his striped prisoner's hat. In his hand are gripped two sausages. Marianne turns and sees Fania, but turns back and continues with the man who is looking straight up at Fania.

Cut to

The dayroom. Through the window the first light of dawn. Backing, we find Fania with several pages of completed score under her hand . . . exhausted, but finishing it. She is fighting self-disgust; at the same time is glad at her accomplishment. A hand enters shot, with a piece of sausage held between forefinger and thumb. Fania looks at it.

Pull back to

Marianne, standing beside Fania, offering the piece of sausage. Fania stares at it, then up at Marianne.

> MARIANNE
> Take it—for saving my life. You must be starved, working all night.

Fania is not looking at her judgmentally but with sorrow and fear. Marianne sets the piece of sausage on the keyboard.

I'm not going to live to get out of here anyway.

But if you do? Marianne? What if you live?

Marianne is silent; then with a certain stubborn air, walks away. Fania looks at the sausage. Tries not to eat it. A desperate struggle to refuse this seeming compromise with her own disgust. Finally she does eat it—and gives way to a look of almost sensual enjoyment as she carefully lengthens out the chewing. Then she swallows, stands in intense conflict, her hands clasped to her mouth as she walks about with no escape.

The sudden sound of ear-piercing whistles.

Fania looks out a window, frightened, bewildered.

Three Blockawas, led by their chief Tchaikowska, come running into the dayroom buttoning up their coats as they rush past Fania into the dormitory.

Cut to

The dormitory. The Blockawas, yelling, *"Raus, raus, schnell . . ."* rip off blankets, push and slap the women out of bed. The women are first in shock, but quickly obey . . . start dressing.

Cut to

The train platform. Dawn. The band is rushed into a formation before a line of freightcars whose doors are shut. SS men stand waiting, also kapos preparing to pounce on the luggage.

Commandant Kramer is standing in open area, beside him Frau Lagerführerin Mandel, in a cape and cap.

Kramer signals Alma, who starts the orchestra in a bright march.

Car doors are rolled open; inside a mass of people who are pulled and driven out onto the platform by kapos, their luggage taken.

Cut to

A mother, being torn from her child which is tossed onto a waiting truck. Mother rushes to Frau Mandel to plead with her; Mandel strikes her across the face with a riding crop.

Cut to

Fania, by the dayroom window. She sees this, starts to turn away in horror, then forces herself to turn back to the window.

Shmuel suddenly appears outside the window and sees her, glances around, then hurries out of sight.

He enters the dayroom. With a glance of caution behind him he hurriedly limps over to Fania.

SHMUEL

Don't do that.

FANIA

What?

SHMUEL

. . . Turn away. You have to look and see everything, so you can tell him when it is over.

FANIA

Who?

55

His eyes roll upward, and he dares point upward just a bit with one finger.

FANIA
FANIA

I don't believe.

A grin breaks onto his face—as though she has decided to play a game with him.

FANIA

Why do you pick me?

SHMUEL

Oh, I always know who to pick!

A crazy kind of joy suffuses his face as he backs out the door.

SHMUEL

Live!

Cut to

The smokestack. Dawn. For an instant the stack is in the clear—then it belches a column of smoke.

Cut to

The dayroom. Evening. Mengele, Kramer and Mandel listen to the orchestra; also their retinues. Fania, accompanying herself, is singing *Un bel di* in an agonized and therefore extraordinarily moving way. She is just finishing. When she does, Mandel stands, she is excited as a patron, a discoverer of talent, and turns to Kramer.

MANDEL

Did you ever hear anything more touching, Herr Commandant?

Fantastic.
(To Mengele)
But Dr. Mengele's musical opinions are more
expert, of course.

Cut to

Fania, staring at the ultimate horror—their love for
her music.

Cut to

The entire dayroom.

MENGELE
I have rarely felt so totally—moved.

And he appears, in fact, to have been deeply stirred.

ALMA
You might thank the Commandant, Fania.

Fania tries to speak, can't and nods instead—gratefully.

FANIA
(Finally a whisper)
Dankeschön, Herr Commandant.

KRAMER
I must tell you, Mademoiselle Fénelon . . .

FANIA
(Uncontrollably)
Excuse me, but my name is really not Fénelon.
Fénelon was my mother's name.

MANDEL

What is your name, then?

FANIA

My father's name was Goldstein. I am Fania Goldstein. Excuse me, I didn't mean to interrupt, Herr Commandant.

KRAMER

You must learn to sing German songs.

ALMA

I will see that she learns immediately, Herr Commandant.

KRAMER

(Continuing to Fania)
Originally, I opposed this idea of an orchestra, but I must say now that with singing of your quality, it is a consolation that feeds the spirit. It strengthens us for this difficult work of ours. *Very* good.

He turns and goes out, followed by his retinue and Mengele. The orchestra is aware Fania has helped them remain in favor and thus alive.

Mandel turns back at the door, beckons to Fania who comes to her.

MANDEL

Is there anything you especially need?

FANIA

(Out of her conflict, after a struggle)
A . . . toothbrush?

MANDEL
(Gestures to Tchaikowska who approaches)
You will send to Canada for some parcels.
(To Fania)
With my compliments.

Mandel exits.

FANIA
(To Tchaikowska)
To *Canada*?!!

Cut to

A long shot of the smoking chimney.

Cut to

A counter set in open air beside another barracks.
Behind it the black market girls—sleek, fed, laughing,
busy trading with a few desperate-looking women
who hand over a slice of bread for a comb or piece of
soap. On the counter are perfumes, lotions, soap and
a pile of used toothbrushes. These "Canadians" all
have hair—Czechs, Poles, Dutch . . .

1ST BLACK MARKETEER
Welcome to Canada. So you're the Frenchy
singer—what would you like?
*(Fania picks up a toothbrush. Charlotte ac-
companies her.)*
That just came off the last transport—it's
practically new and very clean—they were
mostly Norwegians. That'll be a good slice of
bread.

The black marketeer holds out her hand. Fania takes
out a chunk of bread. Laure intercepts, returning
it to Fania.

59

I said this is on the Chief!

BLACK MARKETEER
(Cheerfully)
What's wrong with trying?
(To Fania)
Here's your junk, stupid.

Set aside at one end of the counter are forty tiny packets in soiled and much used paper. Laure and Fania load their arms.

Cut to

The high excitement in the dayroom as the girls open their gift packages which contain, in one case, a bit of butter and a pat of jam which a girl ever so carefully smears on a cracker-sized piece of bread; or an inch of sausage and a chip of chocolate to be savored for a full five minutes.

Marianne, suffering, gobbles up her bread and jam in one gulp.

Fania nearby is swallowing. She takes out her toothbrush.

MARIANNE
You got a toothbrush! —can I see?
(She takes it, examines it, reads words on the handle.)
From Norway. Looks almost new.
(Offering it back)
Nothing like having important friends, right?

Fania's hand stops in air. But then she takes the toothbrush, and forces herself to look directly into Marianne's eyes.

MARIANNE

Whoever that belonged to is probably up the chimney now.
(Fania is silent.)
So why are you superior?

FANIA

If I ever thought I was, I sure don't anymore.

Etalina enters the shot . . . addressing all.

ETALINA

I'll say one thing, Fania—I feel a lot safer now that the Chief is so hot for you.

Some of the women laugh, titillated . . . the Poles loudest of all.

ETALINA

Although I wouldn't want to wake up in the morning next to that Nazi bitch's mug.

FANIA

I don't expect to. But it's not her face that disgusts me.

Esther speaks—a shaven Polish Jewess, angular, tight-faced.

ESTHER

Her face doesn't disgust you?

FANIA

No—I'm afraid she's a very beautiful woman, Esther.

ESTHER

That murderer you dare call beautiful?

Others react against Fania—"Shame!" "You toady!"
"Just because she favors you!"

FANIA

(Overriding)
—What disgusts me is that a woman so beautiful can do what she is doing. Don't try to
make her ugly, Esther . . . she's beautiful and
human. We are the same species. And that is
what's so hopeless about this whole thing.

MICHOU

What's the difference that she's human?
There's still hope—because when this war is
over Europe will be Communist—and for that
I want to live.

ESTHER

No. To see Palestine—that's why you have to
live. You're Jewish women—*that's* your hope;
—to bring forth Jewish children in Palestine.
You have no identity, Fania—and that's why
you can call such a monster human and beautiful.

FANIA

I envy you both—you don't feel you have to
solve the problem.

ESTHER

(Anxiously, aggressively)
What problem! I don't see a problem!

62

She is human, Esther.
> (*Slight pause; she is looking directly into Esther's eyes.*)

Like you. Like me. You don't think that's a problem?

Fania's eye is caught by Marianne slipping out the dayroom door.

Cut to

Outside the barracks, while two kapos expectantly watch, Marianne opens a bar of chocolate they have given her and bites into it. They lead her around the corner of the barracks and out of sight.

Cut to

Fania, asleep in her bunk. Marianne appears, starts to climb in—she is tipsy—slips and lands on her behind on the floor with a scream. Women awaken.

ETALINA

At least let *us* get some rest, Busy-Ass.

MARIANNE

> (*To Etalina*)

What's it to you?

> (*To Fania*)

Say! —Your hair's coming back white!

FANIA

Come to bed, Marianne. . . .

MARIANNE

Oh, screw these idiots. . . .

SHUT UP! WHORE! I'M EXHAUSTED!
SHE'S DISGUSTING! SOMEBODY THROW
HER OUT! SHUT UP!

MARIANNE
(To the whole lot)
Well it so happens, one of them was a doctor
from Vienna. . . .

ETALINA
She just went for a checkup!

MARIANNE
. . . And he thinks we are never going to
menstruate again!
(Silence now)
Because of this . . . this fear every day and
night . . . and the food . . . can sterilize . . .

She looks around at their stricken faces. She climbs up,
helped into her bunk by Fania.

Cut to

A series of closeups:

Esther: (*praying quietly*) Shma Israel, adonai elo-
haynu . . .

Elzvieta: (*crossing herself and praying quietly.*)

Other women praying.

Fania, silent, staring, while beside her Marianne lies
on her back asleep and snoring.

64

Cut to

Two kapos, carrying Paulette on a stretcher across the dayroom to the exit door. Paulette, the young cellist, is in high fever. Alma attempts to explain to kapos in pidgin ...

ALMA

Do you understand me? —she is musician, cellist, not to be gassed. To hospital, you understand? Typhus, you see? We need her. Well, do you understand or not!
(At the door)
Wait!

Cut to

Alma rushing over to Tauber, an SS officer, and Mala. Mala is the tall, striking Jewess, wearing the Star, but who appears to show no obsequiousness toward Tauber, SS officer beside her. Kapos approach carrying Paulette on stretcher.

ALMA

Excuse me, Herr Commandant Tauber—with your permission, would Mala instruct these men to be sure this girl is not . . . harmed? She is our cellist and must go to the hospital— she has high fever, typhus perhaps. I don't know what language they speak. . . .

Without waiting Tauber's permission, Mala stops the kapos.

MALA

Parl' Italiano?
(They nod negatively.)

Espagnol?
    (Nod)
Russky?
    (Nod)

KAPO

Romany.

MALA

Ah!
    (In Roumanian)
Be sure to take her to hospital, not death—
she is a musician, they need her.

KAPO

    (In Roumanian)
We understand.

They walk off with Paulette. Tauber and staff move
off with Mala.

Cut to

The dayroom. The orchestra members are clotted at
the windows watching this.

MICHOU

Isn't she fantastic?—

FANIĀ

    (Amazed)
But she's wearing the Star?

MICHOU

Sure—that's Mala, she's their chief interpreter.
She's Jewish but she's got them bulldozed.

FANIĀ

How's it possible?

66

Alma re-enters the dayroom, goes to her podium, leafs through score.

MICHOU

She's been here for years—since the camp was built—she escaped once; she and five others were supposed to be gassed, so they'd been stripped, and she got out through an air vent. Ended up stark naked going down a road past the Commandant's house. She's afraid of absolutely nothing, so when he stopped her she demanded some clothes; they got to talking, and he found out she speaks practically every language and made her interpreter.

LIESLE

(Proudly)
She's Belgian, you know—like me.

LAURE

She was in the Resistance. She even has a lover.

ETALINA

And handsome!

FANIA

Now you're kidding me.

ETALINA

It's true—Edek's his name—a Polish Resistance guy. He's got a job in the administration.

MICHOU

(Starry-eyed)
They're both unbelievable—they've saved people—a few anyway, and helped some. They're afraid of nothing!

Fania!
> *(From Alma's viewpoint we see the group*
> *turning to her.)*

Come here now and let us go through your
Schubert song.
> *(Fania comes to the piano, sits.)*

You must try the *ch* sound again—Dr. Mengele
has a sensitive ear for the language, and it's
his request, you know. Begin . . .

Fania sings a Schubert song with "lachen" in the verse,
pronouncing "lacken."

ALMA

No-no—not "lacken," —"la*ch*en . . ."

FANIA

> *(Trying, but . . .)*
Lacken.

ALMA

Lachen! Lachen! Lachen! Say it!

Alma's face is close to Fania's; Fania looks into Alma's
eyes and with a sigh of angry defeat . . .

FANIA

Lachen.

ALMA

That's much better. I hope you won't ever be
stupid enough to hate a *language*! Now the
song once more . . . I want you perfect by
Sunday. . . .

Fania, her jaw clamped, forces herself into the song.

Cut to   ￢

The train platform. It is barely light. Freight car doors
roll open, and the deportees are hustled out. From
within the dormitory we hear women yelling and
screaming.

Cut to

The dormitory. Tchaikowska, burly Chief of the Barracks, and other Blockawas are pulling Etalina out of
her bunk by the ankles, and she lands with a bang on
the floor. The other inmates are yelling. . . .

> VOICES
> Why can't you wake up like everybody else!
> Why are you always making trouble! etc. . . .

Alma appears on the scene with Fania nearby.
Tchaikowska bangs a fist on Etalina's back.

> ETALINA
> I said I didn't hear you call me!

> ALMA
> You're a spoiled brat! You will obey, d'you
> hear?

Alma's face is infuriated.

Cut to

Alma's face. She is conducting. Great anxiety about
the sounds coming forth. Suddenly she strides from
the podium to Etalina. She is near hysteria as she
bends over Etalina who looks up at her in terror.

Are you trying to destroy us? That is a B flat;
do you know a B flat or don't you?
(Etalina is cowering in terror.)
I asked if you know B flat or if you do not!

With a blow she knocks Etalina off her chair.

ETALINA
(Screaming—she is a teenager, a child.)
I want my mother! Mama! Mama!

She collapses in tears. Fania goes to her, holds her.

MICHOU
You'd better get some discipline, Etalina.
You're not going to make it on wisecracks.

Alma looks to Fania, a bit guiltily now that her anger
has exploded, then goes out into her own room. Fania
waits a second, then obediently follows her in and
shuts the door.

Cut to

Alma's room. Fania is massaging Alma's shoulders and
neck as she sits in a chair by the window. Alma moves
Fania's fingers to her temples which she lightly massages. After a moment she has Fania massage her
hands, and Fania sits before her doing this.

ALMA
Talk to me, Fania.
*(But Fania keeps silent, wary of expressing
herself.)*
There must be strict discipline. As it is, Dr.
Mengele can just bear to listen to us. If we

fall below a certain level anything is possible . . . He's a violently changeable man.

(But Fania does not respond, only massages.)
—The truth is if it weren't for my name they'd have burned them up long ago; my father was first violin with the Berlin Opera, his string quartet played all over the world. . . .

FANIA

I know, Madame.

ALMA

. . . That I, a Rosé, am conducting here is a . . .

FANIA

I realize that, Madame.

ALMA

Why do you resent me? You are a professional, you know what discipline is required; a conductor must be respected.

FANIA

But I think she can be loved, too.

ALMA

You cannot love what you do not respect. In Germany it is a perfectly traditional thing, when a musician is repeatedly wrong . . .

FANIA

. . . To slap . . . ?

ALMA

Yes, of course! —Fürtwangler did so frequently and his orchestra idolized him.
(Fania keeping her silence, simply nods very slightly.)

71

I need your support, Fania. I see that they look to you. You must back up my demands on them. We will have to constantly raise the level of our playing or I . . . I really don't know how long they will tolerate us. Will you? Will you help me?

FANIA

I . . . I will tell you the truth, Madame—I really don't know how long I can bear this.
(She sees resentment in Alma's eyes.)
. . . I am trying my best, Madame, and I'll go on trying. But I feel sometimes that pieces of myself are falling away. —And believe me, I recognize that your strength is probably what our lives depend on. . . .

ALMA

Then why do you resent me?

FANIA

I don't know! I suppose . . . maybe it's simply that . . . one wants to keep *something* in reserve; we can't . . . we can't really and truly wish to please them. —I realize how silly it is to say that, but . . .

ALMA

But you *must* wish to please them, and with all your heart. You are an artist, Fania—you can't purposely do less than your best.

FANIA

But when one looks out the window . . .

ALMA

That is why I have told you *not* to! You have me wrong, Fania—you seem to think that I

72

fail to see. But I *refuse* to see. Yes. And *you* must refuse!

FANIA

(Nearly an outcry)
... But what ...
(She fears it will sound accusatory.)
... what will be left of me, Madame!

ALMA

Why ... yourself, the artist will be left. And this is not new, is it? —what did it ever matter, the opinions of your audience? —or whether you approved their characters? You sang because it was in you to do! And more so now, when your life depends on it! —Have you ever married?

FANIA

No, Madame.

ALMA

I was sure you hadn't—you married your art. I did marry ...
(Alma breaks off. She moves, finds herself glancing out the window, but quickly turns away.)
... Twice. The first time to that ...
(She gestures ironically toward her violin case lying on her cot.)
The second time to a man, a violinist, who only wanted my father's name to open the doors for him. But it was my fault—I married him because I pitied myself; I had never had a lover, not even a close friend. —There is more than a violin locked in that case, there is a life.

73

FANIA

I couldn't do that, Madame, I need the friend-
ship of a man.

ALMA
(Slight pause)
I understand that, Fania.
(She is moved by an impulse to open up.)
Once I very nearly loved a man. We met in
Amsterdam. The three good months of my
life. He warmed me . . . like a coat. I think . . .
I could have loved him.

FANIA

Why didn't you?

ALMA

They arrested me . . . as a Jew. It still aston-
ishes me.

FANIA

Because your spirit is so German?

ALMA

Yes. It is.
(Slight pause)
In this place, Fania . . . you will have to be
an artist and only an artist. You will have to
concentrate on one thing only—to create all
the beauty you are capable of. . . .

FANIA
(She can't listen further.)
Excuse me, Madame . . .

She quickly pulls open the door and escapes into the
dayroom; Alma is left in her conflict and her anger.
She goes to her violin case on the bed, takes out the

74

instrument. Some emotion has lifted her out of the moment; she walks out of the room.

Cut to

The dayroom. Alma enters; the women come quickly out of their torpidity, reach for their instruments. Alma halts before them and looks out over them. And with an expression of intense pride which also reprimands and attempts to lead them higher, she plays . . . and extraordinarily beautifully, the solo from *Thaïs*, perhaps.

Jew, Gentile, Pole, kapo—Etalina herself and Fania— everyone is captivated, subdued, filled with awe.

As the final crescendo begins—Frau Schmidt and two kapos armed with clubs enter. Everyone leaps up to attention!

FRAU SCHMIDT
Jews to the left, Aryans to the right!

KAPOS
Quick! Hop, hop! Move; quick; five by five!

In the milling around to form two groups, Marianne pushes through and just as the groups make an empty space between them, she pulls an uncomprehending Fania into that space, where they stand alone facing Frau Schmidt.

MARIANNE
She and I are only half.

FRAU SCHMIDT
Half! Half what?

MARIANNE
Half Jewish. Both our mothers were Aryan.

Frau Schmidt's face shows her perplexity as to the
regulations in such cases. Alma steps out of the Jewish
group and goes to her.

ALMA
(Sotto voce, in order not to embarrass her)
Mixed race—are not to be gassed, I'm quite
sure, Frau Schmidt.
*(But Fania overhears and is moved by grati-
tude and surprise.)*
But what is this selection for . . . if I may ask?

FRAU SCHMIDT
(Her hostility to Alma is quite open.)
You belong with the Jews, Madame.
*(Alma steps back into her group, humiliated
but stoic.)*
Jews! Your hair is getting too long! Haircuts
immediately!
(To Fania and Marianne)
You two, follow me!

She makes a military about face and goes out—the
two women follow.

Cut to

A tiny office in the administration building. The over-
stuffed noncom is pouring over a book of regulations
open on a table as Fania and Marianne stand looking
on. He lip-reads, his finger moving along the lines.
Now he finds something, nods his head appreciatively
as he gains his comprehension. Then looks at the
women.

SERGEANT
In this case you are allowed to cut off the
upper half of the Star of David.

Marianne reacts instantly, ripping the star off her coat.
(The Star is actually two separate triangles superimposed.) Fania is uncertain, does nothing.

Cut to

The dayroom. Much agitation: an impromptu sort of
trial is taking place. Sides are taken with Marianne
and Fania alone in the middle.

Fania and Marianne both have half-stars on their
dresses. As they are attacked, Marianne reacts with
far more anguish than Fania who, although disturbed,
is strong enough to remain apart from any group.

ESTHER
You've behaved like dirty goyim, you've dis-
honored the Jews in your families.

MARIANNE
But if it's the truth why should I hide it? I *am*
only half. . . .

ETALINA
Maybe they'll only be half-gassed.

Laughter. Varya, who is standing with other Poles,
steps out of the group.

VARYA
You ashamed to be Jews. You, filth. But you
never be Aryan. God always spit on you. We
Aryan, never you!
        (Spits)
Paa!

Her sister Poles guffaw and heavily nod agreement.

ESTHER

For once the Poles are right!

ETALINA

It's disgusting!—cutting the Star of David in half?

MARIANNE

Why not? —if we can avoid the gas?

FANIA

Since when have you all become such Jewish nationalists? —suddenly you're all such highly principled ladies?

ELZVIETA

Bravo! —You get up on your high horse with them because you don't dare open your traps with anybody else!

FANIA

I'm sorry; your contempt doesn't impress me. Not when you've accepted every humiliation without one peep. We're just a convenience.

ESTHER

The blood of innocent Jews cries out against your treason!

FANIA

Oh Esther, why don't you just shut up? I am sick of the Zionists-and-the-Marxists; the Jews-and-the-Gentiles; the Easterners-and-the-Westerners; the Germans-and-the-non-Germans; the French-and-the-non-French. I am sick of it, sick of it, sick of it! I am a woman, not a tribe! And I am humiliated! That is all I know.

She sits on a chair by the window, her face turned from them. After a silence . . .

> MARIANNE
> You're all just jealous. And anyway, we're just as much betraying the Catholics—our mothers were Catholic, after all.

Fania suddenly gets up and escapes through the door into the dormitory.

Cut to

Fania, seated on a lower bunk, is sewing the upper half of her Star back on. Marianne enters the shot, and behind her some of the other arguers are approaching in curiosity.

> MARIANNE
> What are you doing that for?
> *(Fania is silent)*
> Fania?

> FANIA
> *(Glances up at the group with resentment, then continues sewing.)*
> I don't know. I'm doing it. So I'm doing it.

She sews angrily—at herself too.

Cut to

The barracks "street" outside the dayroom; through windows we see the orchestra and Alma conducting a practice session—phrases are played, then repeated.

79

The rhythm of a passing beam of the arclight which ceaselessly surveys the camp, but here it is only an indirect brightening and darkening.

Coming to the corner of the building, Fania turns into the adjacent street just as a hanging bulb overhead goes out. Shmuel is standing on a short ladder, and descends, leading a wire down with him; he busies himself peeling it back to make a fresh connection. Fania hardly looks at him or he at her, this conversation being forbidden.

The *music* continues in the background from within the dayroom.

SHMUÉL
Behind you, in the wall.

Fania leans against the barracks wall; stuck in a joint between boards is a tiny folded piece of paper which she palms.

FANIA
(A whisper)
Thank you.

SHMUEL
Don't try to send an answer—it's too dangerous; just wants you to know he's here . . . your Robert.
(She nods once, starts to leave.)
Fania? They are gassing twelve thousand a day now.
(Her face drains. He goes up the ladder with wire.)
Twelve thousand angels fly up every day.

80

Why do you keep telling me these things?
What do you want from me!

Shmuel makes the bulb go on, the light flaring on the
wild and sweet look in his face. He looks up.

SHMUEL

Look with your eyes—the air is full of angels!
You mustn't stop looking, Fania!

He perplexes and unnerves her; she claps hands over
her ears and hurries along the barracks wall. As she
turns the corner . . .

She nearly collides with Tchaikowska who is enjoying
a cigarette. She is standing next to the door to her
own room. Fania gives her a nod, starts to pass, when
the door opens; a kapo comes out buttoning his shirt.

TCHAIKOWSKA

Two more cigarettes—you took longer this
time.

KAPO

I'm broke—give you two more next time.

Marianne comes through this door. She is eating meat
off a bone. She sees Fania, is slightly surprised, but
goes on eating. Kapo gives her ass a squeeze and
walks away.

Tchaikowska goes into the room.

Fania sees into the room—Tchaikowska is straightening the rumpled bed.

Cut to

A barracks street. Fania catches up with Marianne, who is stashing the bone with some slivers of meat still on it in her pocket.

> FANIA
>
> At least share some of it with the others—for your own sake, so you don't turn into an animal altogether!

> MARIANNE
>
> Jealous?

She walks away, flaunting her swinging backside, and enters the dormitory.

Cut to

Fania playing the piano with the orchestra. (A light piece, airy, popular music.) The keyboard starts tilting. The orchestra stops, breaking off the music.

Four kapos are turning the piano on its side, onto a dolly.

Fania rescues her music and skitters out of the way, astonished and frightened. Alma and the orchestra look on in silent terror as the piano is simply rolled out of the building through the door to the street.

Does it mean the end of the orchestra? All eyes go to Alma who is clearly shocked and frightened. After a moment . . . as though nothing had happened . . .

> ALMA
>
> Let us turn now to . . . to ah . . .
> *(She leafs through music on podium)*
> the Beethoven . . .

GISELLE

Madame? —if I could make a suggestion . . .

ALMA

I'm sure this will soon be explained . . .

GISELLE

(Desperately)
But why wait till they "explain" it, Madame!
I used to play a lot in movie houses . . . on
Rue du Four and Boulevard Raspail . . . And
I could teach you all kinds of Bal Musette
numbers . . . you know, real live stuff that
won't bore them. I mean, listen just for a
minute!

She plays on her concertina . . . her face perspiring
with anxiety . . . a Bal Musette, lively, dance music. . . .

Enter Frau Lagerfuhrerin Mandel, and Commandant
Kramer, with two SS aides.

All but Giselle spring to attention.

TCHAIKOWSKA

Attention!

Giselle looks up from her concertina and nearly falls
back in a faint at the threatening sight of the big
brass, and stands at rigid attention.

MANDEL

At ease. The officers have decided to keep
the piano in their club for the use of the
members.

KRAMER

(To Alma)

I thought you could manage without it, Madame.

ALMA

Of course, Herr Commandant . . . it was only a little extra sound to fill out, but not imperative at all. We hope the officers will enjoy it.

KRAMER

Which one is Greta, the Dutch girl?

An accordion squeaks . . . it is in Greta's hands.

ALMA

Come!

Greta comes out of the orchestra, accordion in hand. Kramer moves, inspecting her fat, square body. She hardly dares glance at him, her eyes lowered.

KRAMER

Open your mouth.
(In terror she does so. He peers in at her teeth.)
Do you have any disease?

GRETA

(A scared whisper)
No, Herr Commandant.

KRAMER

(To Alma)
Dr. Mengele tells me she's not a very good player.

ALMA

... Not very good, no, although not too bad—
but she ... she works quite hard. ...

KRAMER

But you could manage without her.

ALMA

(Unwillingly)
Why ... yes, of course, Herr Commandant.

Cut to

Fania, flaring with anger at Alma.

Cut to

Kramer, signaling one of the SS aides who steps forward to Greta, preparing to take her off. Greta stiffens.

KRAMER

(To Greta)
My wife needs someone to look after our little
daughters. You look like a nice clean girl.

General relief; Greta is simply rigid. Mandel takes a
coat from the 2nd SS aide and hands it to Greta who
quickly and gratefully puts it on. 1st aide leads her
to exit, and she nearly stumbles in her eagerness to
keep up with him, her accordion left behind.

KRAMER

(Turns to Alma)
This Sunday you will play in the hospital for
the sick and the mental patients. You will have
the Beethoven ready.

ALMA

Yes, Herr Commandant. I must ask your . . .
toleration, if I may—our cellist has typhus and
now without the accordion we may sound a
little wanting in the lower . . .

KRAMER

I will send one of the cellists from the men's
orchestra—they have several from the Berlin
Philharmonic—he can teach one of your violinists by Sunday.

ALMA

*(The idea knocks the breath out of her,
but . . .)*
Why . . . yes, of course, I'm sure we can teach
one of our girls by Sunday, yes.

Kramer turns and strolls out.

MANDEL

*(As though the orchestra should feel hon-
ored)*
It will be very interesting, Madame—Dr.
Mengele wants to observe the effects of music
on the insane.

ALMA

Ah so! —well, we will do our very best indeed.

Mandel walks over to Fania, and pleasantly . . .

MANDEL

And how are you, these days?

FANIA

(Swallowing her feelings)
I am quite well . . . of course, we are all very

hungry most of the time—that makes it difficult.

MANDEL
I offered to send an extra ration this week before the concert on Sunday, but Madame Alma feels it ought to be earned, as a reward afterwards. You disagree?

Fania glances past Mandel to Alma, who is near enough to have overheard as she turns pages in a score. Alma shoots her a fierce warning glance.

FANIA
(Lowering her gaze in defeat)
It's . . . not for me to agree or not . . . with our conductor.

Cut to

Alma's room. Alma is pacing up and down, absolutely livid, while Fania stands with lowered gaze—this could be her end.

ALMA
How do you dare make such a comment to her!

FANIA
I don't understand, Madame—I simply told her that we were hungry. . . .

ALMA
When they have managed to play a single piece without mistakes I will recommend an extra ration—but *I* will decide that, do you understand?
(Fania is silent.)

87

There cannot be two leaders. Do you agree or don't you?

FANIA

... Why are you doing this?

Alma doesn't understand.

FANIA

We are hungry, Madame! And I saw a chance to tell her! Am I to destroy every last human feeling? She asked and I told her!

ALMA

(A bit cowed, but not quite)
I think we understand each other—that will be all now.
(Fania doesn't move.)
Yes? —what is it?

FANIA

Nothing.
(Makes a move to go)
I am merely trying to decide whether I wish to live.

ALMA

Oh come, Fania—no one dies if they can help it. You must try to be more honest with yourself. Now hurry and finish the Beethoven orchestration—we must give them a superb concert on Sunday.

Alma walks to a table where her scores are, and sits to study them. Fania has been reached, and turns and goes out, a certain inner turmoil showing on her face.

Cut to

Etalina, being coached by a young cellist, a thin young man with thick glasses and shaven head. Most of the orchestra is watching them avidly—watching *him*, the women standing around in groups at a respectful distance. The Poles also.

His hands, in close shots, are sensuous and alive and male. The camera bounces such shots off the women's expressions of fascination and desire and deprivation.

Fania tears her gaze from him, and tries to work on her orchestrations—on a table.

Cut to

The cellist's hands. He is demonstrating a tremolo. Etalina tries, but she is awkward. He adjusts her arm position.

Cut to

Paulette, just entering the dayroom from outside. She is barely strong enough to stand. Michou rushes to her with a cry of joy. Fania sees her, and leaps up to go to her; and Elzvieta also and Etalina.

ETALINA
Paulette! Thank God, I don't have to learn this damned instrument!

Cut to

The group helping Paulette to a chair; Paulette is an ascetic-looking, aristocratic young lady.

FANIA
Are you sure you should be out?

89

ELZVIETA

Was it typhus or what?

ETALINA

She still looks terrible.

FANIA

Sssh! Paulette? What is it?

For Paulette is trying to speak but has hardly the
strength to. Everyone goes silent, waiting her words.

PAULETTE

You're to play on Sunday ...

ETALINA

In the hospital, yes, we know.

FANIA

You don't look to me like you should be walking around, Paulette. ...

PAULETTE

*(Stubborn, gallant, she grips Fania's hand
to silence her.)*
They plan ...
   to gas ...
      all the patients ...
         after ...
            the concert.

A stunned silence.

FANIA

How do you know this?

One of the SS women . . .
    warned me . . .
I knew her once . . .
    She used to be . . .
One of the . . .
    chamber maids in our house. So I got out.

Alma enters from her room, sees the gathering, then
sees Paulette.

ALMA

Paulette, —how wonderful! Are you all better
now? —We're desperate for you! —we're doing the Beethoven *Fifth* on Sunday!

Paulette gets to her feet, wobbling like a mast being
raised.

FANIA

She's had to walk from the hospital, Madame
—could she lie down for a bit?

PAULETTE

No! —I . . . I can.

She gets to the cello, sits, as though the room is
whirling around for her. Etalina rushes and hands her
the bow. The orchestra quickly sit in their places.

ALMA

(At podium)
From the beginning, please.

91

The Beethoven *Fifth* begins. Paulette, on the verge of pitching forward, plays the cello. The pall of fear is upon them all now. Fania has resumed her place at the table with her orchestrations. She bends over them, shielding her eyes, a pencil in hand.

She is moved to glance at the window. There, just outside it, she sees . . .

Shmuel, at the window, is pointing at his eyes which he opens extra wide.

Cut to

Fania, startled. Then, lowering her hands from her eyes, forces herself to see, to look—first at Paulette, and the orchestra, and finally at . . .

Alma conducting. She is full of joyful tension, pride, waving her arms, snapping her head in the rhythm and humming the tune loudly, oblivious to everything else.

Cut to

Paulette feverishly trying to stay with the music; her desperation—which those around her understand—is the dilemma of rehearsing to play for the doomed.

Cut to

At one end of the dormitory corridor between bunks, Fania is wringing out a bra and heavy stockings over a pail. Her expression is tired, deadened; she has been changing, much life has gone from her eyes. Nearby, in dimness, Tchaikowska and another Blockawa are lying in an embrace, kissing; Tchaikowska glances over, and with a sneer . . .

Now you do her laundry? —the contessa?

Fania takes the bra and stockings down corridor to
Paulette's bunk, hangs them to dry there. Paulette is
lying awake, but weak.

PAULETTE
Thank you. I'm troubled . . . whether I should
have told the other patients—about what's
going to happen. What do you think?
(Fania shakes her head and shrugs.)
Except, what good would it do them to know?

FANIA
I have no answers anymore, Paulette.

VOICES
Shut up, will you? Trying to sleep! Sssh!

FANIA
Better go to sleep . . .

Across the corridor, Laure is staring at Michou
with something like surprise in her expression, self-
wonder. Michou turns her head and sees Laure staring
at her, and shyly turns away.

Fania now climbs into her own bunk, lies there open-
eyed. Other women are likewise not asleep, but some
are.

Fania lies there in her depression.

She shuts her eyes against the sounds from outside—
the coupling of freightcars, a surge of fierce dogs bark-
ing, shouts—her face depleted. Now Laure's head
appears at the edge of the bunk. Fania turns to her.

Laure timorously asks if she may slide in beside her.

> LAURE

May I?

Fania slides to make room. Laure lies down beside
her.

> LAURE
> *(With a certain urgency)*
> I just wanted to ask you . . . about Michou.

Now their eyes meet. Fania is surprised, curious.
Laure is innocently fascinated, openly in love but
totally unaware of it.

> LAURE

What do you know about her? —I see you
talking sometimes together.

> FANIA

Well . . . she's a militant; sort of engaged to
be married; the kind that has everything
planned in life. Why?

> LAURE

I don't know! She just seems so different from
the others—so full of courage. I love how she
always stands up for herself to the SS.

FANIA
*(Slight pause; she knows now that she is
cementing a relationship.)*
That's what she says about you.

LAURE
(Surprised, excited)
She's spoken about me?

FANIA
Quite often. She especially admired your cour-
age.
(Slight pause)
And your beauty.

Laure looks across the aisle and sees Michou who
is asleep.

Cut to

Michou, emphasizing her hungered look in sleep, her
smallness and fragility.

Cut to

Fania and Laure.

LAURE
She's so beautiful, don't you think? I love her
face.

FANIA
It would be quicker if you told me what you
don't like about her.

LAURE
(Shyly laughs)
I don't understand what is happening to me,
Fania. Just knowing she's sleeping nearby,

95

that she'll be there tomorrow when I wake—
I think of her all day. . . . I just adore her,
Fania.

FANIA

No.—You love her, Laure.

LAURE

. . . You mean . . . ?

FANIA

Why not? She is lovely.

LAURE

I feel . . . I don't know what it is.

Fania softly laughs.

LAURE

Are you laughing at me?

FANIA

After all you've seen and been through here,
you're worried by a thing like that?

LAURE

How stupid I am—I never thought of it as . . .

FANIA

In this place to feel at all may be a blessing.

LAURE

. . . Do you ever have such . . . feelings?

96

(Shakes her head)
I have nothing. Nothing at all, anymore. Go
now, you should sleep.

Laure starts to slide out, then turns back and suddenly kisses Fania's hand gratefully.

FANIA
(She smiles, moved)
What a proper young lady you must have
been!

Laure shyly grins, confessing this, and moves away
down the aisle. She pauses as she starts to pass
Michou. The latter opens her eyes. Both girls stare in
silence at one another—really looking inward, astonished at themselves. Now Michou tenuously reaches
out her hand which Laure touches with her own.

Cut to

Fania, observing them. A deep, desperate concern for
herself is on her face. She closes her eyes and turns
over to sleep.

At the distant drone of bombers, Fania slowly opens
her eyes. Turns on her back, listening.

Cut to

A series of close ups: Michou, Paulette, Liesle, Etalina
. . . and others; they are opening their eyes, listening,
trying to figure out the nationality of the planes.

Now the Polish Blockawas, some in bed with each
other, do the same.

Cut to

Fania. She has gone to a window and is looking out onto the "street." The sound of the bombers continues.

Cut to

The barracks "street." SS guards in uniform carrying rifles—five or six of them converging and looking upward worriedly.

Cut to

Fania, turning from the window and momentarily facing the apprehensive, questioning stares of the Blockawas. She starts to pass them; Tchaikowska reaches out and grasps her wrist.

> TCHAIKOWSKA
> *(Points upward)*
> American? English?
> *(Fania shrugs, doesn't know. Tchaikowska releases her.)*
> Too late for you anyway.

Fania's face is totally expressionless—yet in this impacted look is torment that another human could do this.

> FANIA
> Maybe it is too late for the whole human race, Tchaikowska.

She walks past, heading for the dayroom, not her bunk.

Cut to

Fania, under a single bulb, alone in the dayroom. She has pencil in hand, orchestrating—but she looks off now, unable to concentrate. Elzvieta appears beside her, sits.

ELZVIETA

So it's going to end after all.

(Fania gives her an uncomprehending glance.)

Everyone tries to tell you their troubles, don't they.

FANIA

I don't know why, I can't help anyone.

ELZVIETA

You are someone to trust, Fania—maybe it's that you have no ideology, you're satisfied just to be a person.

FANIA

I don't know what I am anymore, Elzvieta. I could drive a nail through my hand, it would hardly matter. I am dying by inches, I know it very well—I've seen too much.

(Tiredly wipes her eyes)

Too much and too much and too much . . .

ELZVIETA

I'm one of the most successful actresses in Poland.

(Fania looks at her, waiting for the question; Elzvieta, in contrast to Fania, has long hair.)

My father was a count; I was brought up in a castle; I have a husband and Marok, my son who is nine years old.

(Slight pause)

I don't know what will happen to us, Fania— you and I, before the end . . .

FANIA

(With a touch of irony)

Are you saying goodbye to me?

99

(With difficulty)

I only want one Jewish woman to understand
. . . I lie here wondering if it will be worse
to survive than not to. For me, I mean. When
I first came here I was sure that the Pope, the
Christian leaders did not know; but when
they found out they would send planes to
bomb out the fires here, the rail tracks that
bring them every day. But the trains keep
coming and the fires continue burning.—Do
you understand it?—

FANIA

. . . Maybe other things are more important
to bomb. What are we anyway but a lot of
women who can't even menstruate anymore—
and some scarecrow men?

ELZVIETA
(Suddenly kisses Fania's hand)
Oh Fania—try to forgive me!

FANIA

You! —why? What did you ever do to me?
You were in the Resistance, you tried to fight
against this, why should you feel such guilt?
It's the other ones who are destroying us—
and they only feel innocent! It's all a joke,
don't you see? —it's all meaningless, and I'm
afraid you'll never change that, Elzvieta!
(Elzvieta gets up, rejected, full of tears.)
I almost pity a person like you more than us.
You will survive, and everyone around you
will be innocent, from one end of Europe to
the other.

100

Offscreen, we hear the sounds of a train halting, shouts, debarkation noises. Elzvieta turns her eyes toward window.

Cut to

A convoy debarking in the first dawnlight. SS and kapos and dogs.

Cut to

Riven by the sight now, Elzvieta sinks to her knees at a chair, and crossing herself, prays. Fania studies her for a moment . . . then she goes back to work on her orchestration, forcing herself to refuse this consolation, this false hope and sentiment. She inscribes notes. Something fails in her; she puts down pencil.

> FANIA
>
> My memory is falling apart; I'm quite aware of it, a little every day . . . I can't even remember if we got our ration last night . . . did we?

Tchaikowska appears from the dormitory door—she is drinking from a bowl. Now she walks to the exit door of the dayroom, opens it, and throws out the remainder of milk in the bowl, wiping the bowl with a rag.

Elzvieta, still on her knees, watches Tchaikowska returning to the dormitory; she tries to speak calmly. . . .

> ELZVIETA
> You throw away milk, Tchaikowska?

> TCHAIKOWSKA
> It was mine.

ELZVIETA

Even so . . .

TCHAIKOWSKA

Our farm is two kilometers from here—they bring it to me, my sisters.

ELZVIETA

But even so . . . to throw it away, when . . .

She breaks off. Tchaikowska looks slightly perplexed.

TCHAIKOWSKA

You saying it's not my milk?

ELZVIETA

. . . Never mind.

TCHAIKOWSKA
(Taps her head)
You read too many books, makes you crazy.

She exits into dormitory. Elzvieta swallows in her hunger; and, as Fania watches her, she bends her head and more fervently, silently prays.

Cut to

The barracks "street," silent and empty for a moment; suddenly the blasts of sirens, whistles, and the howling of pursuit dogs. From all corners SS guards and dog handlers explode onto the street. They are in a chaotic hunt for someone.

Prisoners are being turned out of barracks onto the "street," lined up to be counted, hit, kicked. . . .

Cut to

The hunters crashing into the dayroom with dogs howling. Blockawas are coming out of the dormitory, throwing on clothes. SS women accompany the guards. Alma comes out of her room questioningly.

Cut to

The orchestra, fleeing from bunks in the dormitory as hunters rip off blankets, overturn mattresses—screaming in fear of dogs, shouting.

Cut to

The players, being driven outside into the "street."

Cut to

The "street." Scurrying to form ranks and trying to dress at the same time the players are calling out their numbers and coming to attention. Before them stand SS officer and dog handler, beside Tchaikowska who is checking off a roster she holds.

Alma stands at attention before the officer.

TCHAIKOWSKA
All accounted for, Mein Herr.

SS OFFICER
(To Madame Alma)
Do you know Mala?

ALMA
Mala? —No, but I have seen her accompanying the Commandant, of course—as interpreter.

SS OFFICER

She has had no contact at all with your players?

ALMA

No-no, she has never been inside our barracks, Herr Captain.

SS officer now walks off, followed by handler and dog. Michou is the first to realize.

MICHOU

Mala's escaped! I bet she's gotten out!

The orchestra is electrified. . . .

LAURE

(To another)
Mala's out!

Blockawas are pushing them back into barracks.

PAULETTE

Fania! —did you hear!

Cut to

The "Canada" girls. Deals are going on at their tables, and a girl prisoner comes hurrying up. A quick whisper to one of the dealers.

GIRL 1

Mala got out . . . and Edek too!

DEALER 1

With Edek? —how!

They got SS uniforms somehow, and took off!

Business stops as three or four dealers cross themselves and bow their heads in prayer.

Cut to

Alma, at the podium going through a score with Fania alongside her pointing out something on it.

The following lines of dialogue are all in close intimate shots—since they dare not too openly discuss the escape. (All are in their chairs, instruments ready for rehearsal.)

LAURE
What a romance! Imagine, the two of them together—God... !

MICHOU
I saw him once, he's gorgeous. Blond, and beautiful teeth ...

LIESLE
She's a Belgian, like me—

ESTHER
What Belgian? —she's Jewish, like all of us ...

LIESLE
Well I mean ...

ELZVIETA
Edek is a Pole, though—and they're going to tell the world what's happening here.

105

Imagine—if they could put a bomb down that chimney!

Now the world will know! Lets play for them... ! The Wedding March!

She raises her violin.

(Readying her bow on the violin—devoutly)
For Mala and Edek!

Mala and Edek!

Etalina, on key for once, readies her instrument.

Cut to

Shmuel, bowing to Alma, his toolbox on his shoulder.

I'm supposed to diagram the wiring, Madame I won't disturb you.

Alma nods, lifts her baton, and starts the number.

Shmuel, as the number proceeds, has a piece of paper on which he is tracing the wiring. He follows along one wall to the table in a corner of the room, where Fania is seated with a score she is following, pencil in hand.

Fania senses Shmuel is lingering at a point near her; and as he approaches her, his eyes on the wiring, he exposes the palm of his hand for her to read. She glances at Alma at the end of the room, then leans a little . . .

Cut to

The palm, reading:

"ALLIES LANDED IN FRANCE."

Shmuel's hand closes.

Cut to

Shmuel, taking his toolbox and slinging it onto his shoulder, hurriedly limps away from the stunned Fania and goes out the exit without turning back.

Fania turns and looks out the window, and sees . . .

The by-now familiar arrival of new prisoners as seen from the dayroom window. Shmuel walks out of the shot, his place taken by . . .

Mandel—who is leading Ladislaus, a four year old boy, away from his mother who is at the edge of a crowd of new arrivals, watching, not knowing what to make of it. The mother now calls to him; we can't hear her through the window. Ladislaus is beautiful, and Mandel seems delighted as she gives him a finger to hold onto.

Note: The character of this particular crowd of prisoners is somewhat different—they are Polish peasant families, not Jews. They are innocently "camping" between barracks buildings, far less tensely than the Jews on arrival, and the kids are running about playing, even throwing a ball. Infants are suckling; improvised little cooking fires; etc. . . . So that Ladislaus' mother is only apprehensive as she calls to him, not hysterical at his going off with Mandel.

Cut to

The orchestra, continuing to play. Etalina is turning with a look of open fear from the window; she leans to Elzvieta beside her and unable to contain herself, whispers into her ear.

Alma sees this breach of discipline and . . .

ALMA

> *(Furiously)*
Etalina!

The music breaks off.

ETALINA

> *(Pointing outside)*
Those are Poles not Jews . . . they're Aryans, Madame!

MICHOU

Why not? —Hitler always said they would kill off the Poles to make room for Germans out there.

ETALINA

But look at them, there must be thousands . . . they'd never gas that many Aryans!
> *(To Alma)*
I think they're going to give them these barracks, Madame!

Mandel and Ladislaus enter.

Silence. Mandel now picks up Ladislaus to show him off to the orchestra.

108

Isn't he beautiful?

Only Tchaikowska and other Blockawas purr and smile. The orchestra sits in silence, not knowing what to make of this or Etalina's theory.

MANDEL
(To Alma)
What's the matter with them?

ALMA
It's nothing, Frau Mandel—there seems to be a rumor that these Aryan Poles will be given our barracks....

MANDEL
Oh, not at all, Madame—in fact, I can tell you that there will be no further selections from within our camp. Of course we have no room for new arrivals—so for them ... there will be other arrangements.

Cut to

Fania, turning out toward the window, and sees ...

A line of trucks loading the peasants for gassing.

Cut to

The child's mother being pushed aboard—but now she is fighting to stay off the truck and looking desperately about for her child.

Cut to

Mandel, now fairly surrounded with players who, in their relief, can now express feeling for the beautiful child. Featured here is Marianne who is chanting a nursery rhyme and tickling his cheek. . . .

MARIANNE

Hoppa, hoppa, Ladislaus
Softly as a little mouse . . .

Mandel, with an almost girlishly innocent laugh, presses the child's face against her own. Then putting him down, and bending to him, holding his hand.

MANDEL

And now we are going to get you a nice new little suit, and shoes, and a sweet little shirt.
(She gives a perfectly happy, proud glance at the orchestra.)
Work hard now—we are all expecting an especially fine concert for the hospital on Sunday!
(To child)
Come along.

She exits with Ladislaus hanging onto her finger.

Cut to

The "street," teeming with life a few moments before, now totally cleansed of people. Mandel leads the boy so as to avoid the dying embers of cooking fires, other debris left by the crowd, bundles, cookpots, etc. . . .

Kapos are policing up the area, throwing debris into hand-drawn wagons. A kapo picks up a ball, and as Mandel approaches he bows a little and offers it to her. She accepts it and hands it to Ladislaus and walks on, tenderly holding his hand.

110

Cut to

The players, clustered at the door and windows, watching Mandel going away. They are all confused, yet attracted by this show of humanity.

GISELLE
So she's a human being after all!

ESTHER
She is? —where's the mother?

ETALINA
Still—in a way, Esther . . . I mean at least she adores the child.

ESTHER
(With wide look of alarm to all)
What's happening here. . . ?

PAULETTE
All she said was that . . .

ESTHER
(Shutting her ears with her hands)
One Polack kid she saves and suddenly she's human? What is happening here!

From the podium, Alma calmly, sternly summons them with the tapping of her baton.

ALMA
From the beginning, please! We have a great deal to do before Sunday.

Silently they seat themselves. And Beethoven's *Fifth* begins.

Cut to

The searchlight from a tower, sweeping the "street."
Sirens sound and the searchlight is extinguished.

Cut to

Marianne, singing; breaks off as the sirens sound. And
all lights go out.

As the sirens die out, bombers take over.

The players sit waiting in the dark, eyes turned upward toward the sound. As the sound rises to crescendo, Alma exits into her room; and as she is closing
the door she catches Fania's eye. Fania rises, approaches the door.

Cut to

Alma's room. Still in darkness, Alma sits. The bombers
are fading.

> ALMA
>
> I will be leaving you after the Sunday concert,
> Fania.
> *(Fania alerts, surprised.)*
> They are sending me on a tour to play for the
> troops. I wanted you to be first to hear the
> news.
> *(A different camera angle reveals the excite-*
> *ment and pride in her expression.)*
> I am going to be released, Fania! Can you
> imagine it? I'll play what I like and as I like.
> They said . . .
> *(Elated now, filling herself)*
> they said a musician of my caliber ought not
> be wasted here! . . . What's the matter? I
> thought you'd be happy for me.

112

FANIA

Well, I am, of course. But you'll be entertaining men who are fighting to keep us enslaved, won't you.

ALMA

But that is not the point! I . . .
(Only an instant's difficulty)
I will play for German soldiers.

FANIA

(Changing the hopeless subject)
And what about us? —we're going to continue, aren't we?

ALMA

I have suggested you to replace me.

FANIA

(Nods, consenting)
Well . . .
(A move to leave)
I hope . . . it ends soon for all of us.

She turns to grasp the doorknob. Planes are gone now.

ALMA

Why are you trying to spoil my happiness?

Fania turns to her, trying to plumb her.

ALMA

I will be playing for honorable men, not these murderers here! Soldiers risk their lives. . . !

FANIA

Why do you need my approval? —if it makes you happy then enjoy your happiness.

ALMA

Not all Germans are Nazis, Fania! You are nothing but a racialist if you think so!

FANIA

Alma—you are free—what more do you want! I agree, it is an extraordinary honor—the only Jew to play a violin for the German Army! My head will explode... !

She pulls the door open just as SS Frau Schmidt walks up to it. Shock. Schmidt is the powerhouse who runs the clothing depot and who knocked Fania down earlier on for speaking out of line.

ALMA

Why ... Frau Schmidt ... come in ... please!

The lights suddenly go on. All glance up, noting this wordlessly.

SCHMIDT

I wanted to extend my congratulations, Madame Rosé—I have just heard the great news.

ALMA

(Ravished)

Oh, thank you, thank you, Frau Schmidt. This is very moving to me, especially coming from you.

SCHMIDT

Yes, but I always express my feelings. I would like you to join me for dinner tonight—a farewell in your honor?

ALMA

I . . . I am overwhelmed, Frau Schmidt. Of
course.

SCHMIDT

At eight then? —in my quarters.

ALMA

Oh I'll be there . . . thank you, thank you.

Schmidt exits. Now, eyes glistening with joy, Alma
turns to Fania.

ALMA

Now . . . now you see! That woman, I can
tell you, has tried everything to be transferred
. . . she is desperate to get out of here, and
yet she has the goodness to come and wish me
well on my departure.

FANIA

(Stunned)
Well I certainly never expected that of her.
. . . But who knows what's in the human heart?

ALMA

You judge people, Fania, you are terribly
harsh.

Alma is now sprucing herself up for dinner, brushing
her skirt, straightening her blouse. . . .

FANIA

And Mandel saved that child. Maybe they
figure they're losing the war, so . . .

ALMA

(At the height of her hopes for herself)
Why must everything have a worm in it? Why
can't you accept the little hope there is in life?

She is now putting on her coat.

FANIA

I'm all mixed up. Schmidt wanting to get out
is really unbelievable, Alma—she's gotten rich
running the black market; she's robbed every
woman who's landed here . . . every deal in
the place has her hand in it. . . .

ALMA

(Extending her hand)
I am leaving in the morning, Fania—if we
don't see each other . . . Thank you for your
help.

FANIA

(Taking her hand)
You are totally wrong about practically everything, Alma—but I must say you probably
saved us all. And I thank you from my heart.

ALMA

You can thank my refusal to despair, Fania.

FANIA

. . . Yes. I suppose that's true.

Cut to

An honor guard, and SS at attention.

The whole orchestra is filing into this room through a
doorway. They are in their finest; atmosphere is
hushed, eyes widened with curiosity, incredulity at
this whole affair.

For at center stands a coffin, flowers on it, the top open. But the orchestra is ranged some yards from it.

When they have all assembled, enter Commandant Kramer, Dr. Mengele, other brass—

And finally Mandel, her finger in the hand of little Ladislaus who is now dressed in a lovely blue suit, and linen shirt, and tie, and good shined shoes, and holding a teddy bear.

First Kramer, Mengele, Mandel, and the other brass step up and look mournfully into the coffin. Now the orchestra is ordered to pay its respects by a glance from Mandel to Fania.

Cut to

Mandel, her eyes filling with tears.

Cut to

The orchestra. A feeling of communion; they are starting to weep, without quite knowing why.

Cut to

Alma—in the coffin. Fania looks down at Alma dead— she is bewildered, horrified. Then she moves off, her place taken by Paulette, etc. . . . The sound of keening is beginning as they realize it is Alma who has died.

Cut to

The black market. Fania is pretending to trade a thick slice of bread for some soap with chief black marketeer, a brazen girl who is smelling the bread offered.

FANIA

What happened?

117

BLACK MARKETEER

Schmidt poisoned her at dinner.

FANIA

How do you know!

BLACK MARKETEER

They shot her this morning.

FANIA

Schmidt!?

BLACK MARKETEER
(Nods)

Nobody was getting out if she couldn't.
'Specially a Jew.

FANIA

Then she really wanted out!

BLACK MARKETEER

Well, she'd made her pile, why not?

Both their heads suddenly turn to the same direction
at a booming sound in the distance.

BLACK MARKETEER
(Looks questioningly at Fania)
That thunder or artillery?

They both turn again, listening in the midst of the
market.

Cut to

Olga, a Ukranian accordionist, has apparently in-
herited the conductorship; she is robot-like in her arm-

waving as she leads them in the *Fifth* Symphony—but it all falls to pieces, and Fania hurries up to the podium.

OLGA

(Before Fania can get a word out)
No! I have been appointed and I am going to conduct!

FANIA

Now listen to me!

OLGA

No! I am kapo now and I order you to stop interfering!

FANIA

Olga, dear—you can barely read the notes, you have no idea how to bring in the instruments!

OLGA

Go back to your seat!

FANIA

You'll send us to the gas! Mengele will be there on Sunday—he won't stand for this racket—it's nonsensical! —Now let me rehearse, and on Sunday you can stand up in front and wave your arms, but at least we'll be rehearsed!

ETALINA

Hey! —sssh!

All turn to listen . . . once again there is the sound of a distant booming.

ETALINA

God . . . you suppose Mala and Edek found
the Russians and are leading them here?

GISELLE

I bet! That was artillery, the Russians are
famous for their artillery. . . !

OLGA

All right, listen! —
*(She is desperately trying to fill out an
image of authority.)*
I know a number. It's very famous with us in
the Ukraine. We are going to play it. First I.

Olga takes up her accordion and launches into a
"Laughing Song," a foot-stomper polka, full of "Ha-
ha-ha, hee-hee-hee," etc.

Orchestra looks at her, appalled, some of them starting to giggle.

Blockawas led by Tchaikowska appear and, loving it,
begin doing polka with one another, hands clap-
ping. . . .

There is sharp whistling outside.

Tchaikowska hurries out into the "street" as players go
to the windows. . . .

Cut to

A gallows. The hanging of Mala and Edek. They have
both been horribly beaten, can barely stand. Mala
stumbles to her knees but flings away the hand of the
executioner and stands by herself under the noose.

The camera now turns out . . . picking up the immense crowd of prisoners forced to watch the executions.

Cut to

Prisoners, en masse. In fact, this was the whole camp, tens of thousands, a veritable city of the starved and humiliated, ordered to watch the execution. This is a moment of such immense human import—for one after another, in defiance, they dare to bare their heads before the two doomed lovers and create a sea of shaven heads across a great space, while SS men and kapos club at them to cover themselves.

Cut to

The gallows—and the drop. Both Mala and Edek are hanging.

Cut to

The sky.

Dissolve from

Sky to rain.

Cut to

The dayroom at night. Rain is falling on the windows. Girls are practicing in a desultory way, breaking off in mid-note to talk quietly together. Fania is at her table; she is playing with a pencil, staring at nothing, her face deeply depressed, deadened.

Now Michou, who is at another window a few yards away, calls in a loud whisper . . .

                    (Pointing outside)
          Fania!

Fania looks out her window.

Cut to

Marianne, on the "street," just parting from the executioner, a monstrous large man, who grimly pats her
ass as she rushes into this barracks.

Cut to

Marianne, entering the dayroom from outside, shaking
out her coat, and as she passes Michou . . .

                    MICHOU
               With the executioner?

Marianne halts. All around the room the expressions
are angrily contemptuous, disgusted.

                    MICHOU
          He killed Mala and Edek, did you know?

                    MARIANNE
          Well if he didn't, somebody else would've,
          you can be sure of that.

She starts toward the door to the dormitory, then
halts, turns to them all.

                    MARIANNE
          I mean to say, dearies, whose side do you
          think *you're* on? Because if anybody's not sure
          you're on the side of the executioners, you
          ought to go out and ask any prisoner in this
          camp, and they'll be happy to tell you!
                    (To Michou)

So you can stick your comments you know exactly where, Michou. Any further questions?

She looks about defiantly, smiling, exits into the dormitory, removing her coat.

The truth of her remarks is in the players' eyes, which avoid one another as the women resume practicing.

Esther comes to Fania.

> ESTHER
>
> You shouldn't let her get away with that. —I'd answer but nobody listens to what *I* say. . . .

> FANIA
>
> But she's right, Esther, what answer is there?

> ESTHER
>
> I am *not* on their side—I am only keeping myself for Jerusalem.

> FANIA
>
> Good.

> ESTHER
>
> *(Fania's uninflected, sterilized comment leaves her unsatisfied.)*
> What do you mean by that, Fania?

> FANIA
>
> That it's good, if you can keep yourself so apart from all this. So clean.

> ESTHER
>
> *(Asking, in a sense)*
> But we're not responsible for this.

123

Of course not, nothing here is our fault.

(Finally agreeing, as it were, to go into it)
All I mean is that we may be innocent, but we have changed. I mean we know a little something about the human race that we didn't know before. And it's not good news.

ESTHER

(Anxiously, even angry)
How can you still call them human?

FANIA

Then what are they, Esther?

ESTHER

I don't like the way you . . . you seem to connect such monsters with . . .

Suddenly, Giselle calls out sotto voce—she is sitting with Laure.

GISELLE

Mengele!

Dr. Mengele's importance is evident in the way they leap to their feet as he enters. His handsome face is somber, his uniform dapper under the raincoat which he now opens to take out a baton and Alma's armband, which has some musical insignia on it.

OLGA

(At rigid attention)
Would the Herr Doctor Mengele like to hear some particular music?

Mengele walks past her to the door of Alma's room.

Cut to

Mengele, entering Alma's room. He looks about at the empty bed and chair, as though in a sacred place. Then he takes the baton and hangs it up from a nail in the wall above a shelf, and on the shelf he carefully places her armband. Now he steps back and facing these relics stands at military attention for a long moment.

The camera turns past him to discover, through the doorway to the dayroom, Fania looking in, and others jammed in beside her, watching in tense astonishment.

MENGELE

Kapo!

OLGA
(Rushing into room)
Herr Doctor Mengele!

She goes to attention.

MENGELE
That is Madame Rosé's baton and armband. They are never to be disturbed.
(He faces the relics again.)
In Memorium.

Fania, as do others nearby, greets this emotional display with incredulity.

Now the dread doctor turns and walks into the dayroom, the players quickly and obsequiously making way for him, and standing with attentive respect as he goes by.

As he passes into the center of the dayroom, his heels clacking on the wooden floor in a slow, pensive measure, the tension rises—no one is sure why. And he halts instead of leaving them, his back to them. Why has he halted, what is the monster thinking?

Cut to

The players. They have risen to a dread tension, their faces rigid.

Cut to

Mengele. He turns to them; he has an out-of-this-world look now, an inspired air, as though he had forgotten where he was and only now takes these faces into consciousness. He seems less angry than alarmed, surprised.

Fania, unable to wait for what may come out of him, takes a tenuous step forward and bows a little, propelled by her terror of death, now, at this moment.

FANIA

> If the Herr Doctor will permit me—the orchestra is resolved to perform at our absolute best, in memory of our beloved Madame Rosé.

Only now does Mengele turn that gaze on her, as though he heard her from afar. Fania's voice is near trembling.

FANIA

> I can assure the Herr Doctor, that we are ready to spend every waking moment perfecting our playing. . . . We believe our fallen leader would wish us to continue . . .
> *(Beginning to falter)*
> to . . . to carry on as she . . . inspired us. . . .

The sound of bombers overhead. Mengele reacts, but in the most outwardly discreet way, with an aborted lift of the head. But the girls understand that he knows the end is near, and this heightens their fear.

He changes under this sound from the sky, and rather strolls out as though to show unconcern. Instantly he is out of sight several girls break into weeping. Fania feels humiliated, and goes alone to her table. . . .

ETALINA

(*Weeping*)
It's the end! You felt it, didn't you, Fania! —he's going to send us to the gas!

PAULETTE

(*Asking Fania's reaction*)
—The way he stared at us!

LAURE

The thing to do is rehearse and rehearse and rehearse!
(*To Liesle*)
To this day you've never gotten the Beethoven right! Now here, damn you! —
(*She thrusts a mandolin at her.*)
work on that arpeggio!
(*She notices Fania looking upward.*)
What's the matter?

The whole group turns to Fania questioningly—they are scared, panicked. She is listening to the sky.

FANIA

I can't understand why they don't bomb here? They could stop the convoys in one attack on the rails.

They're probably afraid they'll hit *us*.

It's political—it always is—but I can't figure out the angles.

They don't want it to seem like it's a war to save the Jews.
(They turn to Esther.)
They won't risk planes for our sake, and pilots—their people wouldn't like it.
(To Fania)
Fania . . . if they do come for us and it's the end . . . I ask you not to do that again and beg for your life. . . .

(Guiltily)
I was only . . .

(Crying out—a kind of love for Fania is in it)
You shouldn't ever beg, Fania!

Cut to

Lagerführerin Mandel entering from the rain. She wears a great black cape. She looks ravaged, desolate. She goes to a chair and sits, unhooks her cape. In one hand now is seen . . .

The child's sailor hat. It is held tenderly on her lap.

Cut to

Mandel, in a state of near shock; yet an air of self-willed determination too, despite her staring eyes.

128

Olga, now the kapo, looks to Fania for what to do. Others likewise glance at her. Fania now comes forward and stands before Mandel.

Mandel comes out of her remoteness, looks at Fania.

> MANDEL
> The Duet from *Madame Butterfly*. You and the other one.

Fania turns to the girls—Giselle hurries into the dormitory, calling...

> GISELLE
> *(Running off)*
> Marianne? Come out here ...!

Mandel now stands and walks to a window looking out at the rain. Meanwhile Laure has taken up her violin to accompany, and Etalina her violin.

Marianne, half asleep, enters from the dormitory and comes to Fania. And now they wait for Mandel to turn from the window and order them to begin. But she doesn't. So Fania walks across the room to her.

Cut to

Fania, arriving beside Mandel who is staring out at the rain-washed window. Fania's eyes travel down to the hat in the other woman's hand.

> FANIA
> We are ready to begin, Frau Mandel.

Mandel seems hardly to have heard, keeps on staring. After a moment...

129

Is something the matter with the little boy?

Mandel now glances at Fania—there is an air of dissociation coming over the Nazi's face.

MANDEL
It has always been the same—the greatness of a people depends on the sacrifices they are willing to make.

Fania's expression of curiosity collapses—she knows now.

MANDEL
I gave him ... back.

Now Mandel is straightening with an invoked pride before Fania, stiffening. But she is still struggling with an ancient instinct within her.

MANDEL
Come now, sing for me.

She goes to her seat. Fania, nearly insensible, joins Marianne—who greets her with a raised eyebrow to keep their hostility intact. Laure's violin starts it off, the Duet from Act II.

SUZUKI (MARIANNE)
It's Daylight! Cho-Cho-San.

BUTTERFLY (FANIA)
(Mimes picking up an infant, cradling it in arms.)
He'll come, he'll come, I know he'll come.

SUZUKI (MARIANNE)
I pray you go and rest, for you are weary. And
I will call you when he arrives.

BUTTERFLY (FANIA)
(To her "baby" in arms)
Sweet thou art sleeping, cradled in my
heart ...

Cut to

Mandel, stunned by the lyric and music; but through
her sentimental tears her fanatic stupidity is emerging.

BUTTERFLY (FANIA)
(Voice over)
Safe in God's keeping, while I must weep
apart. Around thy head the moon beams
dart....

Cut to

The group.

BUTTERFLY (FANIA)
(Rocking the "baby")
Sleep my beloved.

SUZUKI (MARIANNE)
Poor Madame Butterfly!

Cut to

Mandel, fighting for control, staring up at Fania. And
Fania now takes on a challenging, protesting tone.

BUTTERFLY (FANIA)
Sweet, thou art sleeping, cradled in my heart.
Safe in God's keeping, while I must weep
apart.

131

The sound of bombers . . . coming in fast, tremendous.

Sirens.

Mandel comes out of her fog, stands . . . girls are rushing to windows to look up. The lights go out.

The sound of bombers overhead and nearby explosions.

There is screaming; in the darkness, total confusion; but Mandel can be seen rushing out into the night, a determined look on her face.

Cut to

The railroad platform. Bombs explode in the near distance.

Despite everything, deportees are being rushed onto waiting trucks which roar away.

Cut to

A series of close shots: Kramer kicking a deportee.

Mandel commanding a woman to board a truck.

And Mengele, face streaming, his eyes crazed as he looks skyward; then he goes to an SS officer.

MENGELE
Hurry! —faster!

Cut to

The warehouse hospital. *The Blue Danube* is in full swing as the shot opens. At one end of the vast shadowy space is the orchestra "conducted" by Olga. The few good violinists like Elzvieta and Charlotte saw away as loudly as possible.

132

The Beckstein piano has been brought in and Fania is playing.

The sick, what appear to be hundreds, are ranged in beds; the insane, some of them clinging to walls or to each other like monkeys; about a hundred so-called "well prisoners" in their uniforms ranged at one end . . . dozens of SS officers, male and female, in one unified audience sit directly before the players.

Cut to

A dancing woman emerging from among the insane; heads turn as she does a long, sweeping waltz by herself; shaven-head, cadaverous, a far-out expression. SS glance at her, amused.

Cut to

The prisoners. A humming has started among them to *The Blue Danube*.

Cut to

Mengele, Kramer and SS officers. These high brass notice the humming—they take it with uncertainty—is it some kind of demonstration of their humanity?

Cut to

The prisoners. They have dared to hum louder—and the fact that it is done in unison and without command or authorization enlivens them more and more.

Cut to

Commandant Kramer, starting to get to his feet when Mengele touches his arm and gestures for him to permit the humming as harmless. Kramer half-willingly concedes, and sits.

Cut to

The orchestra. *Blue Danube* ends. With no announcement, in the bleak silence, Olga picks up her accordion. Fania and Paulette immediately come to her and have a quick whispered conversation while trying to appear calm.

> FANIA
> *(Sotto voce)*
> Not the "Laughing Song"!

> OLGA
> But they want another number!

> PAULETTE
> But they're all going to the gas, you can't play that!

> OLGA
> But I don't know any other! What's the difference?

Olga steps from them and begins to play and sing the "Laughing Song" which requires all to join in.

And as it proceeds, some of the insane join in, out of tempo to be sure, and . . .

Kramer is laughing, along with other SS.

Patients in beds are laughing. . . .

Cut to

Fania: In her eyes the ultimate agony.

134

Cut to

Mengele, signaling Kramer, who is beside him, and the latter speaks to an aide at his side. The aide gets up and moves out of the shot. . . .

Cut to

The orchestra. The "Laughing Song" is continuing.

Cut to

A door to the outside is opening and kapos are leading half a dozen patients through it.

Cut to

The orchestra. The "Laughing Song" continues; now Paulette sees the kapos leading people out. Her cello slides out of her grasp as she faints. "Laughing Song" is climaxing. Michou is propping up Paulette while attempting to play and laugh.

Cut to

The warehouse hospital. Patients, orchestra and SS are rocking along in the finale, as more patients are being led out through the door.

Cut to

The dayroom. Later that night. The players are sitting in darkness while some are at the windows watching a not very distant artillery bombardment—the sky flashes explosions.

Fania, seated at her table, is staring out window. She is spiritless now.

Players' faces—in the flashes of light from outside, are somber, expectant.

Cut to

A fire in the dayroom stove, visible through its cracks. Michou is grating a potato into a pan. Laure is hungrily looking on. This is very intense business.

Cut to

Olga, the new conductor, emerges from Alma's room: She is very officious lately.

                    OLGA
All right—players? We will begin rehearsal.
    (*Heads turn to her but no one moves.*)
I order you to rehearse!

                    ETALINA
    (*Indicates outside*)
That's the Russian artillery, Olga.

                    OLGA
I'm in charge here and I gave no permission
to suspend rehearsals!

                    ETALINA
Stupid, it's all over, don't you understand?
The Russians are out there and we will prob-
ably be gassed before they can reach us.

                    GISELLE
Relax, Olga—we can't rehearse in the dark.

                    ETALINA
She can—she can't read music anyway.

                    OLGA
    (*Defeated, she notices Michou.*)
Where'd you get those potatoes?

MICHOU

I stole them, where else?

OLGA
(Pulls her to her feet)
You're coming to Mandel! —I'm reporting
you!

From behind her, suddenly, Fania has her by her hair.

FANIA
(Quietly)
Stop this, Olga, or we'll stuff a rag in your
mouth and strangle you tonight. Let her go.

Olga releases Michou.

LAURE
She was only making me a pancake, that's all.

FANIA
Sit down, Olga—we may all go tonight.

OLGA
I don't see why.

ETALINA
We've seen it all, Dummy, we're the evidence.
(Olga unhappily stares out a window.)
I feel for her—she finally gets an orchestra to
conduct and the war has to end.

Cut to

A series of close shots:

The players' faces—the exhaustion now, the anxiety,
the waiting.

137

Cut to

Etalina, just sitting close to Fania.

> ETALINA
>
> I think I saw my mother yesterday. And my two sisters and my father.

> FANIA
>
> *(Coming alert to her from her own preoccupations)*
>
> . . . What? —Where? What are you talking about?

> ETALINA
>
> Yesterday afternoon; that convoy from France; when we were playing outside the freight car; I looked up and . . . I wasn't . . . I wasn't sure, but . . .

Their eyes meet; Fania realizes that she is quite sure, and she reaches around and embraces Etalina, who buries her face in Fania's breast and shakes with weeping.

> FANIA
>
> Oh, but what could you have done?

Cut to

Lagerführerin Mandel, entering the dayroom. All rise to stand at attention, faces flaring with anxiety. Mandel is wide-eyed, totally distracted, undone. Etalina is weeping as she stands at attention.

> MANDEL
>
> Has anyone come across that little hat?
> *(Silence. No one responds. Amazement in faces now.)*

138

The little sailor hat. I seem to have dropped it. —No?

Heads shake negatively, rather stunned. Mandel, expressionless, exits.

The players sit again.

Etalina has an explosion of weeping.

FANIA
(*Comforting her*)
Sssh . . .

Marianne now comes over to Fania, who is stroking Etalina's face.

MARIANNE
I just want you to know, Fania, that . . . you turned your back on me when I needed you, and . . . I don't want you to think I'm too stupid to know it.

FANIA
What are you talking about?
(*Marianne bitterly turns away, as . . .*)
Are you a little child that I should have locked in the closet?

Marianne walks away to a window, adamantly bitter.

Cut to

Michou, feeding Laure pieces of pancake from a pan, as she would a child.

Cut to

Fania, looking with a certain calculation at . . .

Elzvieta, who blanches and turns from an explosion in the sky, and crosses herself.

Fania comes up to her.

FANIA

Elzvieta? —
(She takes out a small but thick notebook.)
I would like you to keep this. It's my diary—everything is in there from the first day.

ELZVIETA

. . . No-no, you keep it. You will be all right, Fania. . . .

FANIA

Take it. Take it, maybe you can publish it in Poland. . . .

ELZVIETA

(Starts to take it, then doesn't)
It's impossible, Fania—I feel like I'm condemning you! You keep it, you will live, I know you will!

FANIA

I am not sure . . . that I wish to, Elzvieta.

ELZVIETA

(Realizing, she looks deeply into Fania's dying eyes.)
Oh no . . . no, Fania! No!

She suddenly sweeps Fania into her arms, as . . .

Two troopers enter. These are not SS men; they carry rifles and combat gear.

140

1ST TROOPER
Jews left! Aryans right! Hurry up!

The players scurry to form up. . . .

Fania and Elzvieta slowly disengage—it's goodbye.

Cut to

An open freight car. Dawn is breaking; rain drenches some twenty-five players in this freight car ordinarily used for coal. Fania, now, is lying on her back with eyes shut, the players extending their coats to shield her. The train slows.

Nearby two Wehrmacht troopers are huddled over a woodstove; women also cluster around for warmth. These men are themselves worn out with war, dead-eyed.

Marianne makes her way over to one of the troopers and gives him a flirty look.

MARIANNE
How's it going, soldier?

The trooper's interest is not very great.

MARIANNE
Could a girl ask where you're taking us?

She comes closer—and with mud-streaked face, she smiles. . . . Now he seems to show some interest in her.

MARIANNE
Cause wherever it is, I know how to make a fellow forget his troubles. —Where are we heading?

141

TROOPER

(Shrugs)
Who knows? —I guess it's to keep you away
from the Russians, maybe . . . so you won't
be telling them what went on there. Or the
Allies either.

MARIANNE
Going to finish us off?

TROOPER
Don't ask me.

The train stops.

Cut to

A flat, barren, endless landscape covered with mud.

Cut to

An SS officer mounting onto the car; below him on
the ground are several other SS plus dogs and
handlers.

The officer looks the players over, then points at
Marianne. She steps forward. He hands her a club.

SS OFFICER
You are the kapo. Get them out and formed
up.

Officer hops down and moves off to next car.

Cut to

Marianne, who hefts the club in her hand and turns
to the players, who all seem to receive the message
her spirit emits—they fear her.

Out, and form up five by five.

She prods Paulette in the back as she is starting to
climb down.

PAULETTE
Stop pushing me!

Marianne viciously prods Paulette who falls to the
ground as Michou and Giselle seek to intercede; and
Marianne swings and hits Giselle, then goes after
Michou, and both escape only by jumping down and
falling to their hands and knees. Now Marianne turns
to the *pièce de résistance*—

Fania is practically hanging from the supporting
hands of Laure and Etalina who are moving her
past Marianne.

MARIANNE
She can walk like anybody else.

ETALINA
She's got typhus, Marianne!

She beats their hands away from Fania who faces her,
swaying with a fever. Marianne swings and cracks
Fania to the floor of the car.

Cut to

A vast barn or warehouse, its floor covered with hundreds of deportees in the final stages of their physical
resistance. They are practically on top of one another;
and over all a deep, undecipherable groaning of
sound, the many languages of every European nation.

Now a shaft of daylight flashes across the mass as a
door to the outside is opened and through it a strag-
gling column of deportees moves out of this building.
The door closes behind them, followed by . . .

The sound of machine guns.

Cut to

The little group of players around Fania are wide-
eyed, powerless. She is propped up in Paulette's lap
now, panting for breath.

Fania opens her eyes . . .

> ETALINA
> *(Slapping Fania's hands)*
> That's better . . . keep your eyes open . . .
> you've got to live, Fania. . . .

Now Fania, half-unconscious, sees past Etalina . . .
to . . .

A woman and man making love against a wall.

A man barely able to crawl, peering into women's
faces, calling:

> "Rose? Rose Gershowitz?"

Cut to

A Polish woman, surrounded by the ill and dying,
giving birth, with help from another woman.

Machine guns fire in near distance. Along with the
baby's first cries.

Cut to

Fania, receiving these insanely absurd sounds with a struggle to apprehend. And now she sees . . .

The Polish woman who just gave birth, standing up, swaying a little, wrapping her rags about her as she takes her baby from a woman and holds it naked against herself.

Cut to

Fania, ripping the lining out of her coat—which was lying on top of her as a blanket—and gestures for Paulette to hand it on to the Polish woman, which is done. And the baby is wrapped in it.

Light again pours in from the opening door, and another column of deportees is moving to exit and death. And as this column stumbles toward the door, urged on by SS men and kapos . . .

Cut to

Shmuel, who appears in the barn door. The light behind him contrasts with the murk within the building and he seems to blaze in an unearthly luminescence. He is staring in a sublime silence, as now he lifts his arms in a wordless gesture of deliverance, his eyes filled with miracle, and turning he starts to gesture behind him. . . .

A British soldier appears beside him and looks into the barn.

Cut to

The British soldier. His incredulous, alarmed, half-disgusted, half-furious face fills the screen.

Cut to

A panoramic shot: A shouting mass of just-liberated deportees throwing stones. Some of these people are barely able to stand, some fall to their knees and still throw stones at . . .

Truck filled with SS men and women, their arms raised in surrender, trying to dodge the stones. Several trucks are pulling away, filled with SS.

Fania is being half-carried by Michou and Etalina, the others near them.

> ETALINA
> Please, Fania, you've got to live, you've got to live. . . !

Michou suddenly sees something offscreen, picks up stones and starts throwing. . . .

> MICHOU
> There she is! Hey rat! Rat!

Paulette and Esther turn to look at . . .

Marianne.

In the midst of the mob, Marianne is being hit by stones thrown by Michou. Other deportees are trying to hold on to Marianne to keep her from escaping. . . .

> FANIA'S VOICE
> *(Offscreen)*
> Michou!

Michou turns to . . .

Fania, steadied on her feet by the others, staring at . . .

146

Marianne, frightened, but still full of defiant hatred.

Cut to

A British communications soldier with a radio unit, coming up to Fania.

> SOLDIER
> Would it be at all possible to say something for the troops?

Fania registers the absurdity of the request.

> SOLDIER
> It would mean so much, I think . . . unless you feel . . .

She stops him by touching his arm; all her remaining strength is needed as she weakly sings *The Marseillaise*.

> FANIA
> *Allons enfants de la Patrie*
> *Le jour de gloire est arrivé*
> *Contre nous de la tyrannie . . .*

Fania's eyes lift to . . .

The sky. The clouds are in motion.

Cut to

A busy, prosperous avenue in Brussels—1980 autos, latest fashions on women, etc. . . .

Cut to

A restaurant dining room. The camera, so to speak, discovers Fania at a table, alone. It is a fashionable restaurant, good silver, formal waiters, sophisticated lunch crowd. Fania is smoking, sipping an aperitif, her eye on the entrance door.

Of course she is now thirty-five years older, but still vital and attractively done up, and dressed. And she sees . . .

First Liesle, the miserable mandolin player, who enters and is looking around for her. Fania half-stands, raising her hand. As Liesle starts across the restaurant toward her, Laure enters behind her. And she recognizes Liesle.

Keeping Fania's viewpoint—Laure quickly catches up with Liesle, touches her arm; turns; a pause; they shake hands, then Liesle gestures toward Fania's direction and they start off together.

Cut to

Liesle and Laure arriving at table; Fania is standing; a pause. It is impossible to speak. Finally, Fania extends both her hands, and the other two grasp them.

FANIA

Liesle!—Laure!

They sit, their hands clasped. After a moment . . .

LIESLE

We could hardly believe you were still singing—and here in Brussels!

LAURE

I'm only here on a visit, imagine?—And I saw your interview in the paper!

148

Words die in them for a moment as they look at one another trying to absorb the fact of their survival, of the absurdity of their lives. Finally . . .

FANIA

What about the others? Did you ever hear anything about Marianne?

LIESLE

Marianne died.

FANIA
(It is still a shock.)
Ah!

LIESLE

A few years after the war—I can't recall who told me. She was starting to produce concerts. She had cancer.

LAURE

I have two children, Fania . . .

FANIA

Laure with children!—Imagine!

A waiter appears. He knows Fania.

WAITER

Is Madame ready to order or shall we . . . ?

FANIA

In a few minutes, Paul.
(With a glance at the other two)
We haven't seen each other in thirty-three years, so . . . you must ask the chef to give us something extraordinary; something . . . absolutely marvelous!

149

And she reaches across the table to them and they clasp hands.

Cut to

Their hands on the white tablecloth, and their numbers tattooed on their wrists.

The camera draws away, and following the waiter as he crosses the restaurant, we resume the normality of life and the irony of it; and now we are outside on the avenue, the bustle of contemporary traffic; and quick close shots of passersby, the life that continues and continues. . . .

Final fade-out.

ABOUT THE AUTHOR

ARTHUR MILLER was born in the Harlem section of Manhattan in 1915 and attended public schools there. He attended the University of Michigan where he wrote two plays a year and was rewarded with several prizes and awards. On his return to New York after graduation he continued to write plays and worked in radio. In 1949 *Death of a Salesman* received the Pulitzer Prize. His next major play was *The Crucible* (1953), followed by *A View from the Bridge* (1955), which received the Gold Medal Award for Drama from the National Institute of Arts and Letters. Mr. Miller's other works include *After the Fall* (1964), *Incident at Vichy* (1964), *The Price* (1968), *I Don't Need You Anymore*, a book of short stories (1967), *The Creation of the World and Other Business* (1972), *Theatre Essays* (1978), *Chinese Encounters* (with Inge Morath, 1979), and *The American Clock* (1980).

DISCOVER
THE DRAMA OF LIFE
IN THE LIFE OF DRAMA

☐	13434	**CYRANO DE BERGERAC** Edmond Rostand	$1.75
☐	12204	**FOUR GREAT PLAYS** Henrik Ibsen	$1.95
☐	13615	**COMP. PLAYS SOPHOCLES**	$2.95
☐	13307	**FOR COLORED GIRLS WHO HAVE CONSIDERED SUICIDE WHEN THE RAINBOW IS ENUF** Ntozake Shange	$2.50
☐	14559	**MODERN AMERICAN SCENES FOR STUDENT ACTORS** Wynn Handman	$3.50
☐	11936	**FOUR GREAT PLAYS BY CHEKHOV** Anton Chekhov	$1.75
☐	14674	**THE NIGHT THOREAU SPENT IN JAIL** Jerome Lawrence and Robert E. Lee	$2.25
☐	13390	**RUNAWAYS** Elizabeth Swados	$2.50
☐	12832	**THE PRICE** Arthur Miller	$1.95
☐	13363	**BRIAN'S SONG** William Blinn	$1.95
☐	14678	**THE EFFECTS OF GAMMA RAYS ON MAN-IN-THE-MOON MARIGOLDS** Paul Zindel	$2.25
☐	14161	**50 GREAT SCENES FOR STUDENT ACTORS** Lewy Olfson, ed.	$2.50
☐	12917	**INHERIT THE WIND** Lawrence & Lee	$1.75
☐	13102	**TEN PLAYS BY EURIPIDES** Moses Hadas, ed.	$2.50
☐	13902	**THE CRUCIBLE** Arthur Miller	$2.25
☐	14689	**THE MIRACLE WORKER,** William Gibson	$2.25
☐	14101	**AFTER THE FALL** Arthur Miller	$2.50

Buy them at your local bookstore or use this handy coupon for ordering: